Rosalind Horton | Sally Simmons

111 Places
in Cambridge
That You
Shouldn't Miss

Photographs by Guy Snape

emons:

Bibliographical information of the Deutsche Nationalbibliothek
The Deutsche Nationalbibliothek lists this publication in
the Deutsche Nationalbibliografie; detailed bibliographical data
are available on the internet at http://dnb.d-nb.de.

© Emons Verlag GmbH
All rights reserved
© Photographs by Guy Snape, except:
The Busway (ch. 17), photo: mauritius images/Alamy;
Clough Gates (ch. 29) by kind permission of the Mistress
and Fellows of Newnham College; Kettle's Yard (ch. 59) c. 18th Venetian Mirror,
Kettle's Yard House, University of Cambridge, photo: Paul Allitt;
Lawrence Room (ch. 61) by kind permission of the Mistress and
Fellows of Girton College, University of Cambridge;
Museum of Zoology (ch. 75) by kind permission of the University
Museum of Zoology; Stapleford Granary (ch. 101),
photo: Gillies Adamson Semple;
Grand Arcade (ch. 105), photo: Philip Moore.
© Cover icon: Illustration: Elena Rosa Gil
Design: Eva Kraskes, based on a design
by Lübbeke | Naumann | Thoben
Maps: altancicek.design, www.altancicek.de
Printing and binding: Grafisches Centrum Cuno, Calbe
Printed in Germany 2024
First edition 2017
ISBN 978-3-7408-2376-4
Revised seventh edition, October 2024

Guidebooks for Locals & Experienced Travellers
Join us in uncovering new places around the world at
www.111places.com

Foreword

Cambridge is not a big city, even taking its urban sprawl into account, and the historic town centre is very small, with an area of only 0.5 square miles. It's tempting to try to 'do' Cambridge in an afternoon, and indeed many people do – King's College Chapel, a punt up the river, a pint in a pub, a quick nip into the shops and away again. This means that for most of the year Cambridge is packed, with coachloads of visitors, pavements full of shoppers and streets full of bikes. When the University students are up (and there are over 20,000 of them) the town never seems still or empty.

Cambridge has changed enormously in the many years that we have lived and worked here, a period in which the extraordinary growth of new high-tech companies has had the biggest impact on the town since the founding of the University 800 years ago. Employment and wealth have transformed the city; property prices are among the highest in the country, there is a lot of regrettable new building and the traffic is dreadful. And yet in essence Cambridge is unchanged. It has always been a place where odd and peculiar people and things can be accommodated comfortably, and although the pull of history is strong, it has never held back innovation and experimentation.

We imagine that, like us, you will probably realise that the best way of getting around the city is by bike and the easiest way of exploring is on foot, especially in the centre, where even finding a place to park your bike can be a problem. And we hope you have as much fun exploring Cambridge as we have had photographing and writing about the places in this book.

111 Places

1_ Abbey House

Cambridge's most stately home

Few people travelling along the noisy and very unlovely Newmarket Road out of Cambridge realise that just over 20 yards down an unassuming side street stands a veritable stately home that is the oldest continuously inhabited house in the city.

Abbey House was built on land that belonged to Barnwell Priory, which was founded in 1092, although it seems to have had no connection with it. There are a few visible reminders of Barnwell Priory: the wall around the garden was partially built from stones that belonged to the Priory, and in the garden (just visible through the gates from the road) are two rustic arches. The house dates from around 1580, although it was extended in 1678, and was owned by a succession of Cambridge worthies, including 'Polite' Tommy Panton, Lady Gwydir and Joseph Sturton, whose names live on in the area.

In 1945 the property, by now very dilapidated, was bought by Lord Fairhaven of Anglesey Abbey, who gave it to the Cambridge and County Folk Museum. Although repairs were carried out on it, none of their plans ever came to anything (high winds caused it to creak alarmingly, most likely giving rise to the tales of hauntings). They passed it on to the city council who rented it out, its last tenants being Professor Peter Danckwerts, a brilliant international scientist, who had been a wartime bomb disposal officer, and his wife. On their deaths the council put the house up for sale; it was acquired by the Friends of the Western Buddhist Order, and is now occupied by a residential spiritual community. For some time they opened the house one day a year for guided tours, but sadly this no longer happens, so visitors can only gaze across the garden and imagine the history hidden behind the walls. And now only the small handful of residents who live there can say if the ghostly nun, disembodied head or spectral animals still haunt the house.

Address Abbey Road, CB5 8HQ | **Getting there** Citi 3 to Newmarket Road / Ditton Walk or buses 10, 10A, 11, 12 or 17 to Elizabeth Way | **Hours** Viewable from the outside only | **Tip** Nearby, in Beche Road, are the remains of Barnwell Priory. Only the old storehouse, called the Cellarer's Chequer, survives; it can be viewed from the outside.

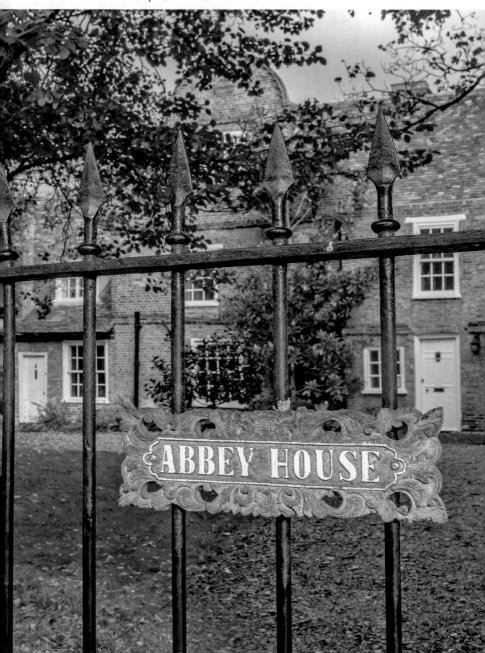

2__ The ADC Theatre
A springboard to stardom

In 1855 the new Cambridge University Amateur Dramatic Club made its home in the old coaching inn off Jesus Lane that is now known simply as the ADC. The University disapproved; performances were often halted by the Proctors, and the number of productions was strictly limited. Today, things are very different. The theatre is now a department of the University, which runs it on behalf of the club.

From the start, the club attracted high-profile undergraduates, among them the future King Edward VII. Finances were strained, the theatre was unheated, war and fire interrupted the club's activities, but from 1935 plays were staged almost continuously. The club's earliest productions were light comedies, but a serious interest in drama soon began to emerge among its members. The Marlowe Society was the first company to stage little-known works by Christopher Marlowe (after whom it was named) and neglected Jacobean playwrights. Later, the revues produced by the Cambridge Footlights kick-started the satire boom of the 1960s, making household names of those who took part. Two decades later, another generation of students, including Stephen Fry, Hugh Laurie and Rowan Atkinson, similarly revolutionised British comedy.

The roll call of actors, directors, writers and comedians who cut their teeth at the ADC includes some of the best-known names in entertainment and public life, from theatrical knights and dames (Ian McKellen, Derek Jacobi, Peter Hall, Trevor Nunn, Julian Fellowes, Emma Thompson) to Oscar winners, TV and radio stars, novelists and politicians.

In 2011 the ADC took over the Corpus Playroom in St Edmund's Passage, a smaller space. Between them, the venues stage two weekly main shows, late shows and one-off productions. Whatever you choose to go and see, make sure you hang on to your programme. The names inside could become award winners in the not-too-distant future.

Address Park Street, CB5 8AS, +44 (0)1223 300085, www.adctheatre.com | **Getting there** Any Citi bus (1–8) to town centre; Grand Arcade car park | **Hours** See website for details of productions | **Tip** Ignore its underwhelming situation next to the new development – The Maypole pub is a delightful free house with a wide selection of real ales and beers from local breweries. Run by the same Italian family for 35 years, it has a cosy interior and a large covered outside space. Unsurprisingly, its pizzas are very popular.

3_ All Saints' Church

A masterpiece of Victorian Gothic Revival

Once considered one of the finest Victorian churches ever built, by 1973 All Saints' future hung in the balance. In that year, the vicar retired and the parish was merged with that of the Round Church. For years the church stood empty, grass growing high outside and damage caused by neglect spreading inside; by 1979 it was threatened with demolition. A campaign to save it was mounted by local and national conservation groups, not without controversy: some people felt that the money needed for restoration should go to help the living, not empty churches. But saved it was, and since 1981 it has been cared for by the Churches Conservation Trust, which has put into place a programme of restoration.

Its exterior is grey and rather uninviting and, despite its great size, many people manage to pass by it without even noticing that it is there. Inside, it's neither the altar nor even the paintings that will draw your attention, magnificent though they certainly are; it's the walls. George Bodley, one of the finest church architects of his generation, drafted in leading Victorian artists to work on the interior, and they were joined by craftsmen from Frederick Leach's City Road workshop, including David Parr (see ch. 36). When the church was built in 1870, William Morris was commissioned to produce the design for the east end of the church. Here you can see the huge, intricate stencilled patterns against a deep, rich background. Elsewhere, Leach and his son painted much of the rest, which is a riot of pomegranates and flowers. The stained glass windows, so dull from the outside, shine like jewels from within the church. The East Window, which shows figures from the Old Testament, is a Pre-Raphaelite masterpiece displaying the work of William Morris, Edward Burne-Jones and Ford Maddox Brown.

Long closed but now open to all, All Saints' is most definitely worth a visit.

Address Jesus Lane, CB5 8BP, +44 (0)20 7213 0660, www.thepaintedchurch.co.uk | Getting there Citi 1, 1A, 2, 3 or 8; Grand Arcade car park | Hours Currently no fixed opening hours, but regular organised events ensure that the church is open for visitors (see website). Guided tours for groups of 10 or more are available by arrangement. | Tip Next door to All Saints' is the theological college Westcott House, established in 1881 for the training of Anglican ministers. The peaceful and attractive grounds are open to the public.

4_ The American Cemetery

'In proud memory of their valor'

Off the Madingley Road, just as you think you have left Cambridge behind, is the American Cemetery. Constructed from soft Portland stone, the memorial is bright rather than dazzling, and simple rather than stark. But the dignified and stirring language of the tributes to the fallen inevitably brings a lump to the throat. The site evokes the indomitability of the human spirit even while acknowledging the enormous sacrifice of servicemen and women during World War II.

The Wall of the Missing, the longest in any war cemetery, lists the names of more than 5,000 members of the army, navy, air force and coastguard lost in action, with statues representing each of the four services. Among the names are those of Glenn Miller and Joseph P. Kennedy Jr, as well as that of Leon Vance, highlighted in gold, a documented hero and the recipient of the US Medal of Honor. Their stories, and those of many less well known, are told in the excellent Visitor Center to the west of the site.

The chapel to the east of the site has breathtaking mosaics by Francis Scott Bradford, showing angels escorting aircraft heavenward and images of resurrection. One entire wall is a map showing the campaigns in Europe and the Atlantic, with ships and planes sculpted in silver and gold.

More than 11,000 US servicemen and women were interred in the cemetery during the war. Many were killed during training exercises, including the infamous Exercise Tiger on the Devon coast, a rehearsal for the D-Day landings in which nearly 800 US soldiers were killed by friendly fire or ambushed by German ships. After the war, the US government repatriated bodies at their families' request. Now there are nearly 4,000 graves, which continue to be visited by relatives and descendants. They are laid out in a radial pattern from the focal point of the flagpole, where the Stars and Stripes flies permanently.

Address Madingley Road, Coton, CB23 7PH, +44 (0)1954 210350, www.abmc.gov/
cemeteries-memorials/europe/cambridge-american-cemetery | **Getting there** Hop-on Hop-off
bus from Drummer Street. By car: A1303, direction Coton/St Neots | **Hours** Daily 9am–5pm
including UK bank holidays (except 25 Dec and 1 Jan) | **Tip** Nearby Madingley Hall isn't
open to the public, but you can visit the lovely gardens, designed by Capability Brown in
1756. Waymarked paths show them at their best. Guides are available from the reception.

5 Anna Maria Vassa Memorial

'But one, a hapless orphan, slumbers here'

High on the wall just by the entrance to St Andrew's church is a rather grand memorial to a young girl who died in 1797, aged four. That she should be remembered in this way is testament to the esteem in which her father was held, and the story behind his life is an extraordinary one.

Her father was Olaudah Equiano, kidnapped from his village in Nigeria at the age of 11 and carried off into slavery. He was bought by a Captain Pascal, who named him Gustavus Vassa and brought him back to England. He learned to read and write and eventually bought his freedom. Living in London, he became active in the anti-slavery movement and was championed by the Revd Dr Peckard, Master of Magdalene College, Cambridge, who was also prominent in the campaign against slavery. It is likely that Peckard encouraged Equiano to write his life story.

'I believe there are a few events in my life, which have not happened to many.' So Equiano began his tale, which was published in 1789 under the title *The Interesting Narrative of the Life of Olaudah Equiano, or Gustavus Vassa, the African.* One of the first widely read slave accounts, the book became a bestseller, and was reprinted eight times in his lifetime.

Equiano may have met his future wife, Susannah Cullen, who came from Fordham in Cambridgeshire, through his contact with Revd Peckard. They were married in 1792 and set up home in Soham, not far from her home village. The following year Anna Maria was born, followed in 1795 by her sister, Joanna, but the family's joy was short-lived: tragedy struck when in February 1796 Susannah died, aged 34. The following year Equiano died, in London, and just a few short months after that Anna Maria too was dead.

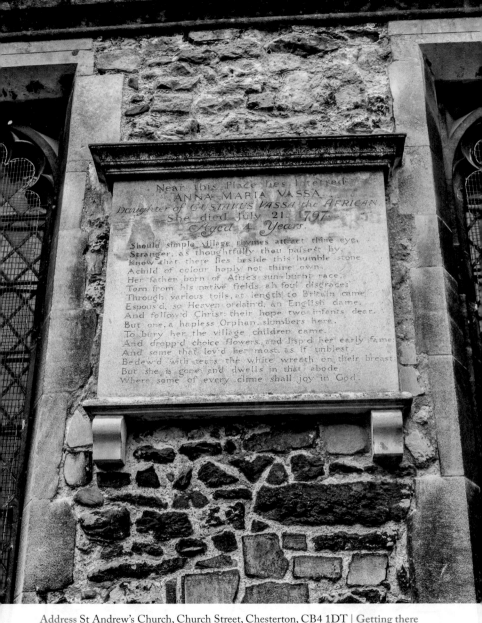

Near this Place lies interred:
ANNA MARIA VASSA
Daughter of GUSTAVUS VASSA the AFRICAN
She died July 21 1797
Aged 4 Years.

Should simple village rhymes attract thine eye,
Stranger, as thoughtfully thou passest by,
Know that there lies beside this humble stone
A child of colour haply not thine own.
Her father born of Afric's sun-burnt race,
Torn from his native fields, ah foul disgrace:
Through various toils, at length to Britain came
Espous'd, so Heaven ordain'd, an English dame,
And follow'd Christ: their hope two infants dear.
But one, a hapless Orphan, slumbers here.
To bury her the village children came,
And dropp'd choice flowers, and lisp'd her early fame,
And some that lov'd her most, as if unblest,
Bedew'd with tears the white wreath on their breast:
But she is gone, and dwells in that abode,
Where some of every clime shall joy in God.

Address St Andrew's Church, Church Street, Chesterton, CB4 1DT | **Getting there** Bus 117 or Citi 2 to Chesterton High Street | **Hours** Daily 9.15am–4pm for visits; Sun services 8am & 10am | **Tip** From Church Street, walk down almost to the end of Chapel Street where you will come across Chesterton Tower, built in the mid-14th century. The land on which it stands was sold off for housing in the 1960s, leaving the tower incongruously stranded next to a row of garages.

6_ Arjuna Wholefoods
Doing you good, naturally

The striking yellow exterior and profusion of herbs outside Arjuna hint at the good things to come inside. When it opened in 1970, the facts behind what we eat were largely unknown and not such a concern for most people. Today, with so much processed food, people want to know something about what they are consuming, and this small, vibrant store that stocks 100 per cent vegetarian food is hugely popular in the local community.

Back in the 1970s, wholemeal bread was still a rarity and the UK's best-known vegetarian restaurant was even called Cranks. Arjuna's founders were fired with an idealistic desire to spread the word about vegetarian wholefood – and to enjoy themselves in the process. They set themselves up as a co-operative, with everyone participating equally in decisions – something that continues to this day. The small premises soon attracted like-minded people and became a hub for those seeking new social and spiritual directions.

In the beginning, food was packed in the shop, but as trade expanded Arjuna took over a unit in Dale's Brewery. This enabled them to increase the floor space of the shop and to begin wholesaling to colleges and other outlets. Everything was, and still is, packed by hand in their warehouse in biodegradable plastic.

Today, the shop sells thousands of lines, from dry goods to organic fruit and vegetables. It keeps its carbon footprint low with the principle of 'local, national, overseas', in that order. There are big jars of dried herbs, spices and teas that customers can weigh themselves and put into bags (brown paper, naturally). Herbal remedies, biodegradable cleaning products and natural cosmetics appear alongside superfoods like quinoa (of which Arjuna stocks three kinds), cereals and pulses, rice, non-dairy yogurt, cheese and ice cream, and a variety of breads, from sourdough to gluten-free. Try the vegan lunch or one of their incredible superfood salads.

Our fruit and vegetables
are **Organic** and locally
sourced whenever
possible.
We think you'll find it's the
widest range in Cambridge!

organic fruit & v

URCED FROM LOCAL PRODUCERS WHENEVER POSSIE

35p each   Apricots £7.80 Peach   Kiwi 25p each   Nectarine 95p each   Lemons 59p   Avocado

re-tomato
£4.65k   Mixed cherries £6.49k   £4.35 box   broad
                                                                                           beans
                                                                                           £2.30kg

New Potatoes
£1.15 KG

25 each
n - £2.50 each   Aubergines £5.18 kg   Shallots £4.29 KG

Address 12 Mill Road, CB1 2AD, +44 (0)1223 364845, www.arjunawholefoods.co.uk |
Getting there Citi 2 to Mill Road, opposite Mortimer Road | **Hours** Mon–Sat
9.30am–6pm, Sun 11.30am–5pm | **Tip** Many of Cambridge's best charity shops can be
found on the same side of the road as Arjuna, selling clothes, second-hand furniture and
bric-à-brac, all at reasonable prices.

Marrow £1.50kg   Kale £1.35 bag   Red

7_ Art at Addenbrooke's

More pictures than patients

Never mind that Addenbrooke's has a worldwide reputation as a teaching hospital and centre of medical excellence. Leave aside the advances it has made in organ transplantation, neurology, cancer, midwifery and paediatrics. The really big thing at Addenbrooke's is art. The hospital has turned its corridors into galleries, and has even found room for a museum to celebrate its 250-year history. As a result there are more works of art in the hospital than patients, and it is all funded through fundraising and charitable donations.

The long corridor that links the Outpatients' Department and the Treatment Centre, crossing the main concourse, is the principal exhibition space, and the one most easily accessed by patients and visitors. Exhibitions are regularly hung here, with all proceeds going to the art fund, and there are permanent displays of paintings, drawings and installations. Winning entries from staff competitions also find space on the walls. The collection brings together work by well-known professional artists, like Quentin Blake, and paintings by famous surgeons, like the transplant pioneer Sir Roy Calne. Opposite a bank of lifts is a wall of stunning floor-to-ceiling mosaics by Jim Anderson, showing scenes of daily life. The *joie de vivre* and detail in these could keep you rooted to the spot for hours – but there are those lifts behind you…

In fact, browsing is not the keynote of a visit to the Addenbrooke's art collection, unless you are lucky enough to hit a quiet period, a rare thing in a huge modern hospital, and of course corridors must not be blocked. It is difficult to linger anywhere for long, so you will probably need to make several passes at the museum's exhibits to appreciate them fully.

It's well worth it, however. Having lovely things to look at in hospital corridors and wards improves the well-being of patients, staff and visitors.

Address Hills Road, CB2 0QQ, +44 (0)1223 245151, www.cuh.nhs.uk | Getting there
Most buses from the city centre and to or from Babraham Road Park & Ride; by car, ideally
use the Park & Ride; there is a charge for parking on the hospital site | Hours As for the
Outpatients' Department | Tip On the south-west side of the Addenbrooke's site you can
pick up the DNA Cycle Path, which runs alongside the railway from the hospital to Great
Shelford. Part of the national cycle network, the path is painted with over 10,000 coloured
stripes and represents just one of the genes in the human genome. Look out for the double
helix structures at either end.

8 Arts Picturehouse

The phoenix rises, again

In 1997 the curtain finally fell at the ABC Cinema, then the name for the magnificent Regal picture palace, which had first opened its doors in 1937. Competition from the new Warner multiplex cinema in the Grafton Centre had taken its inevitable toll.

Cambridge had always been rich in cinemas, but the Regal remained the biggest and the best, showing the latest films before any of the others. When major releases came out, queues would build up early and snake around the front, right down the side passageway to the back of the cinema. From the 1950s it was also the venue for a string of rock and pop acts that included Cliff Richard, Billy Fury and a band that was still relatively unknown – the Beatles.

Somewhat more modest in scale, the original Arts Cinema in Market Passage opened in the 1930s as the Cosmo. Loved dearly by its countless fans, it had many quirks and faults: smelly drains, poor heating, no disabled access, noise from outside during particularly gripping scenes and – perhaps more critically – no bar. Its closure in 1999 was greeted with howls of protest, and promises to open a bigger and better cinema back on the old Regal site were met with scepticism.

But the critics were proved wrong. The site was acquired by pub chain J. D. Wetherspoon, who spent £1.8 million converting part of the former cinema into a pub. Up above, on the site of the old cinema's restaurant, the Arts Picturehouse was born. With three screens, comfortable seating for 500 and an attractive 1930s-style bar area, the cinema became an immediate success. Art house films, and live screenings of opera and ballet, appear happily alongside more mainstream offerings. State-of-the art projection equipment ensures the best possible experience: there are fewer than 30 cinemas in the UK with 70-millimetre projection capability, and the Arts Picturehouse is proud to be one of them.

Address 38–39 St Andrew's Street, CB2 3AR, +44 (0)871 902 5720, www.picturehouses.com | Getting there Citi 1, 2 or 3 to Emmanuel Street; Grand Arcade car park | Hours Daily; see website for show times | Tip Take the glass-backed lift to the top floor in the nearby John Lewis department store for a delightfully revealing, if brief, view over Emmanuel College.

9 Ascension Parish Burial Ground

Genius beneath our feet

The Ascension Burial Ground on Huntingdon Road was originally Cambridge's country churchyard, opened when the cemeteries in town began to run out of room. The poet Thomas Gray imagined country churchyards housing 'some mute inglorious Milton' but there is nothing inglorious about the clamorous reputations of those buried here. The graves contain the remains of some of the greatest intellectuals of the 19th and 20th centuries.

It is easy to miss the entrance to the cemetery, which lies at the end of a surprisingly long track. This leads to a deconsecrated chapel used by the letter cutter Eric Marland as a studio. The cemetery opens out from this point. It is a modest and strangely neglected place compared with the great cemeteries of Highgate in London and Père Lachaise in Paris, although it can boast almost as many world-famous scientists, astronomers, historians, writers and thinkers.

The roll call of the great minds interred among the 1,500 graves is impressive. It includes 3 Nobel Prize winners, 8 members of the Order of Merit, 22 knights and 9 Masters or Principals of Cambridge colleges. A panel shows where some of their graves can be found. Scientific, academic and social revolutions can be traced through the names of those buried here. They include several members of the Darwin family, but the most-visited grave is that of Ludwig Wittgenstein – a plain, flat stone on which people sometimes leave strange and touching tributes, all of which Eric Marland collects and archives. It is odd to think that this philosopher and mathematician has become the Jim Morrison of the cemetery.

The burial ground is now a City Wildlife Site within a conservation area, and it is managed carefully to maximise the diversity of the plant species found there and to maintain the graves themselves.

Address All Souls' Lane, Huntingdon Road, CB3 0EA, +44 (0)1223 315000 | Getting there Citi 5 or 6 from town centre to Storey's Way or All Souls' Lane | **Hours** Daily 9am – 5pm | **Tip** Head up Huntingdon Road then left into Eddington to any of the numerous cafés and restaurants that have sprung up around the market place.

10 The Bells of Great St Mary's

Ring the changes with Cambridge Surprise Major

To reach the top of Great St Mary's tower, you have to brave a narrow, winding medieval turret staircase of 123 steps. This is not for the claustrophobic or those with vertigo, but if you do make it to the top, you will be rewarded with one of the best views of the city and countryside beyond. On your way up, you will pass the ringing room and the bell chamber – places that offer a glimpse into the history of the bells that have been a part of the church since 1303. Bells have been rung at the church to call people to services, to announce births, marriages and deaths, and to mark momentous national events.

Change ringing, part team sport and part mathematical pattern, originated in England in the early 17th century. A new way of hanging bells was devised that involved mounting the bell on a wheel with the rope passing around it, allowing for much more control of the bell's movement. Ringing bells in sequence is what distinguishes the English style from bell ringing in other parts of the world, where the sounds are more random.

The Society of Cambridge Youths are the band of volunteer ringers responsible for making sure that the changes are rung. Because of the way the bells revolve, it is not possible to play tunes, but using what bell ringers call the 'Method' (the sequences they must all learn off by heart) they can play intricate runs of notes.

In 1793 a new clock was commissioned and a chime specially composed. Known as the 'Cambridge Quarters', this chime was copied in 1859 for the new bells and clock in the Palace of Westminster, where Big Ben hangs, and where the tune is known as the 'Westminster Chimes'. To mark the University's 800th anniversary in 2009, 13 new bells were installed, joining the original clock bells.

ON MONDAY JAN, 21st 1788,
Was rung in this Tower,
A true and exquisite Peal,
consisting of 6600 Changes,
BOB - MAXIMUS,
In 5 Hours and 5 Minutes.
Without a false Change;
BY
The undermentioned
CAMBRIDGE YOUTHS.

Treble. I. SMITH	7th. T. JONES
2d. W. BLAND	8th. P. GOUDE
3d. R. LAUGHTON	9th. C. DAY
4th. J. LAWSON	10th. W. YOUNG
5th. J. COE	11th. J. HAZARD
6th. T. STEERS	Tenor. J. BOWTELL.

J. Willimott ┐ Church
R. Wheeler ┘ Wardens.   Bobs by C. Day

In this Tower
On Monday March 11th 1850,
Was Rung a true & complete Peal of
GRANDSIRE TRIPPLES
Consisting of 5040 Changes,
with 190 Bobs & 50 Singles, in 3
Hours & 24 Minutes. By the un-
-dermentioned Cambridge Youths

Treble	5th
J. LEE.	T. MANSFIELD
2nd	6th
W. PAGE.	R. WILLBY
3rd	7th
F. YORKE.	M. ROCKETT
4th	Tenor
T. WRIGHT.	J. HOLLIDAY

The Peal was Composed by
TAYLOR and conducted by
R. WILLBY

Revd   Caius   Vicar
R. White ┐
S. Howell ┘   Church Wardens

Address Senate House Hill, CB2 3PQ, +44 (0)1223 747273, www.greatstmarys.org |
Getting there Any Citi bus (1–8) to town centre; Grand Arcade car park | **Hours** Tower
Mon–Sat 10am–5.30pm, Sun noon–5pm (last entry to the tower 30 minutes before
close) | **Tip** Behind St Mary's, facing the market, is a rare memorial to the Boer War that
is overlooked by most people. The bronze plaque, which is flanked by two stone soldiers,
remembers the men of Cambridgeshire and the Suffolk Regiment who fought, and died,
during that 1899–1902 war.

11　Betty Wu Lee Garden

How pineapples helped to create a garden

Dr Lee Seng Tee, a wealthy Singaporean investment banker with interests in rubber and pineapple plantations, first visited Wolfson College with his wife in 1973 when their daughter took up a place to study there. By chance, Dr Lee was given a lift to the station by college tutor and plant pathologist Peter Lowings, and during the journey he described the problems he was having with the pineapples on his Malaysian estates, where many plants were collapsing. This aroused the interest of Dr Lowings, who immediately sent some of his research students to investigate. Once there, they discovered that the problem was due to a bacterial infection caused by ants, and things were rapidly put right.

Dr Lee was so grateful for this help that he gave the college the funds to build a library, a hall and a garden. Named after his wife, the small, secluded Betty Wu Lee Garden is tucked well away around the back of the college. It is protected on one side by the hall, built in the Chinese style, and just next to it stands a stone horse from northern China, familiarly known as Henry, which stands on a granite plinth from the old London Bridge. He arrived broken into many pieces, having been dropped in transit, but has been carefully put back together. On the far side of the garden is a replica in miniature of the bandstand in the Singapore Botanic Gardens. At the eastern end of the garden is a colour-washed Chinese-style wall topped by interlocking pantiles, beneath which are several water-carved stones from Lake Tai. The planting in front of the wall includes dwarf pines, willows and bamboo, all designed to move in the breeze and cast interesting shadows. An oriental cedar with fasciated leaves makes shapes against the wall that you might imagine are great mythical beasts from the Orient.

And all over the college, as a reminder of their benefactor, you will find images of pineapples.

Address Wolfson College, Barton Road, CB3 9BB, +44 (0)1223 335900, www.wolfson.cam.ac.uk | **Getting there** Bus 18 or 75 to Grange Road | **Hours** Mon–Sat 9am–6pm; check first at Porters' Lodge | **Tip** Head back towards town and stop off at the Red Bull, a friendly traditional pub selling a wide range of beers and good food.

12 Bin Brook

The other Cambridge river

You have probably walked along or across Bin Brook without even realising it. This unobtrusive little river runs from west to east across Cambridge, passing through Newnham and down to the Backs before slipping into the Cam in two different places. At some places it's a ditch, at others a rather horrid, muddy trickle, and at others a bucolic stream that has been enhanced by sympathetic landscaping. Most of the time its activity is completely innocuous, but Bin Brook has caused serious flooding on many occasions. When it burst its banks in October 2001 several houses and college gardens were flooded, causing considerable damage.

By and large, however, Bin Brook is charming, and following its course can provide a couple of hours' very pleasant diversion – and some detective work. Going downstream, the brook enters Cambridge at the bottom of Cranmer Road, where you catch a glimpse of it before it heads off through grassland and drainage channels until it reappears at Robinson College. Here, Bin Brook has been made the central feature of the college gardens, and retains its character as a rural stream. It's much less lovely where it crosses below Grange Road, but at Burrell's Court in Trinity College it is once again incorporated into the design of a series of beautiful courts and gardens. If you are lucky enough to be there when Trinity opens these gardens to the public, you are in for a treat. Otherwise, it's back to sleuthing to trace Bin Brook down to Queen's Road. Here, it flows in two directions in the system of drainage ditches round the gardens of Trinity and St John's, joining the Cam as it passes through the grounds of both colleges.

Although Bin Brook has been interfered with at many points along its course, for better and for worse, it is still a habitat for sticklebacks, dace, frogs, kingfishers, herons and moorhens, and a variety of wild flowers.

Address A good place to start following the river is at Robinson College, Grange Road, CB3 9AN, +44 (0)1223 339100, www.robinson.cam.ac.uk | **Getting there** Bus 18 to Newnham, opposite Grange Road | **Hours** Robinson College gardens are open to the public all year round | **Tip** Cobbett's Corner is the small triangle of natural woodland crossed by Bin Brook at Grange Road. Owned and maintained by the City Council, it is carpeted with snowdrops and crocuses in the spring.

13 The Blue Ball

Everything you'll ever want from a pub

Take a walk from Cambridge to Grantchester on a winter afternoon, look to your right across Grantchester Meadows and you will see the irresistible sight of the Blue Ball, lit up and drawing you in with its promise of warmth, company, excellent beer and homemade food.

A pub has been on this site for over 250 years, which makes the Blue Ball the oldest pub in Grantchester. The original building was destroyed by fire and rebuilt in the late 19th century. It is likely that its name records the landing of a hot air balloon in the meadow opposite a century earlier. Its owners, Toby and Angela Joseph, bought the delapidated pub in 2014 and run it as a free house, renovating and modernising while retaining the features that make everyone fall for it: log fires, traditional pub games, shelves of books and scrubbed wooden tables where customers rub shoulders with both old and soon-to-be-new friends. The outside space has been designed as a beer garden to provide additional seating and a two-bed self-catering apartment is also available. Dogs are made as welcome as their owners, both outside and in, where there are jars of treats on the bars.

Food is served at lunch and dinner times and everything on the menu is provided by local suppliers and prepared and cooked in the pub kitchen, from filled baguettes to the legendary chilli con carne and shepherd's pie, including vegetarian options. It's not an extensive menu but this is not a gastro pub. You can't make a reservation to eat here but if you want to eat when you come, you will be spoiled for choice from a selection of delicious regular dishes.

The Blue Ball is equally irresistible in the summer, of course, when its outside spaces, with their glorious, OTT hanging baskets, come into their own. And though it's in Grantchester, it's not for nothing that it is considered the best pub in Cambridge by those in the know.

Address 57 Broadway, Grantchester, CB3 9NQ, +44 (0)1223 846004,
www.info@blueballgrantchester.co.uk | **Getting there** On foot via Grantchester Meadows;
by car via Trumpington Road (A1134); bus 18 from city centre | **Hours** Wed–Sat
noon–10pm, Sun noon–7pm | **Tip** The nicest way to reach the Blue Ball is to walk through
Grantchester Meadows from the Millpond in Cambridge (about an hour each way). You can
take the formal footpath or follow a more meandering path alongside the river and imagine
you are following in the footsteps of Byron, Rupert Brooke – or Pink Floyd.

14 Bodies in the Bookshop
It's no mystery – and here's the proof

Whoever said crime doesn't pay? Certainly not book publishers, who have benefited from soaring sales of crime fiction of all kinds: classic detective, hardboiled, domestic *noir*, police procedural and, more recently, cosy crime (think clerics, feisty seniors, baffled police and a dash of humour). The promise of crime is that we will get to find out who dunnit, and maybe even work it out for ourselves – a compelling promise indeed.

One person who has been at the centre of this flourishing genre is Richard Reynolds, until recently head of the crime section at Heffers Bookshop, by far the best and quirkiest crime fiction section in the country. When he wasn't busy selling crime novels, Richard was judging them, having been for several years chair of the CWA Gold Dagger award for best crime novel of the year. His particular passion is the Golden Age of crime fiction; that is, those novels published in England during the 1920s and 1930s, encompassing such *grandes dames* as Agatha Christie, Ngaio March, Margery Allingham and Dorothy L. Sayers. To say his own collection of these books is comprehensive would be something of an understatement, since he's been accumulating them for over 50 years.

Richard is now indulging his passion in the small but perfectly formed Bodies in the Bookshop, which is devoted to selling classic English crime novels – many of them from his own collection. They're arranged by genre, so you can easily work your way through your favourite kind – maybe historical whodunnits, crime in translation, Cambridge crime, Golden Age and that catch-all 'miscellaneous'.

Richard's partner in crime is publisher Jon Gifford, who has an area in the shop devoted to his books, mostly local, such as Whipplesnaith's *The Night Climbers of Cambridge* and Xu Zhimo's selected poems among others.

Not visiting Bodies in the Bookshop would be positively criminal.

Address 1a Botolph Lane, CB2 3RD, +44 (0)1223 485163, www.bodiesinthebookshop.com | Getting there Bus 199, U1 or U2; Grand Arcade car park | Hours Tue–Sat 11am–5pm, Sun noon–4pm | Tip The Anchor, across the road and down Silver Street, is an iconic Cambridge pub with fantastic views of the water from its riverside terrace. Look out for reminders of local boys Pink Floyd.

15 __ The Box Room Café

No time to be board

There's nothing the owners of the Box Room Board Game Café like more than playing board games. As a family, they have always played games, and love anything competitive. They visited many board game cafés in different places, agreeing on what worked well and what didn't. And they had their own ideas about how they would do things better.

So, when a prime site in Cambridge became available, they were on the spot, and prepared to put their ideas into action. Taking all the best aspects of other places and putting them together with their own vision, they came up with The Box Room Café.

With over 550 games available (and growing all the time), it shouldn't be hard to find exactly the one that suits you – from strategy game Agricola and party game Abandon all Artichokes to classic family games like Uly Polly. And just in case you're not the competitive sort, they have co-operative games, so you and your friends can play together but *against* the game. If you have a game languishing at home in the back of a cupboard, you can bring it along and find someone to play it with, or come with a bunch of friends and play against each other. Maybe you've even created a new game? Try it out on members of the public and ask them for their feedback.

The café has a warm and welcoming vibe that's designed to appeal to all age groups. Food is simple and easy to eat while you're busy concentrating on your game – toasties, fries, natchos, burgers. Hot drinks, soft drinks, beer and wine are also available. Customers pay a cover charge for two hours' play, which is reduced if you buy food or drink. Games are changed regularly, and anything damaged or perhaps not quite as popular as anticipated is retired to the basement.

Come on your own for Wednesday's Meet and Mingle. Or perhaps Dungeons and Dragons is more to your taste – played in the basement, naturally.

Address 58 Regent Street, CB2 1DP, +44 (0)1223 662266, www.theboxroombgc.co.uk | **Getting there** Bus 1, 3 or 7 to Downing College; Grand Arcade car park | **Hours** Tue–Thu 2–10pm, Fri 2–10.30pm, Sat noon–10.30pm, Sun noon–9.30pm | **Tip** The Box Room is perfectly located between Lockhouse Escape Games and Warhammer, so you can indulge your thirst for gaming and fantasy by dropping in there.

16 The Brick Tree

A single garden for all the world's habitats

On the south walk of Cambridge's 40-acre Botanic Garden, near to the rose garden, is a most unusual tree. Many people miss it, as it's not a particularly striking specimen; this is a *Pyrus communis*, known as the European or common pear. During a storm in the 1960s, a branch snapped off and, in keeping with the orthodoxy of the time, the gap was filled up with tar-covered bricks to prevent the tree from rotting. Since then, the wound has calloused over and the bricks have become a part of the tree, and it is affectionately known as the Brick Tree.

Unusual specimens abound in this wonderful garden, as you might expect. Look out for *Parrotia persica*, the Persian ironwood tree, with its peculiar fused and twisted branches; and *Metasequoia glyptostroboides*, the dawn redwood or fossil tree – one of the greatest discoveries in the plant world of the last century; Isaac Newton's famous apple tree (or, rather, a scion of the original); and the giant redwoods.

The Botanic Garden owes its existence to the vision of Charles Darwin's mentor and botany tutor John Stevens Henslow, who conceived of this major tree collection. It opened in 1846 and today succeeds in being a perfect blend of recreational facility and serious place of learning, one that supplies material to research scientists across the world. But there is more to this garden than trees: plants that thrive in all manner of habitats have been established here, to instruct and delight – from the Scented Garden and Damp Bog Garden to the dry nooks and crevices of the Rock Garden.

The glasshouses are an especially magical realm, where visitors can make a horticultural voyage through time and across continents to experience the drama of plant diversity for themselves. But not many visitors are lucky enough to be visiting when the stinky 'corpse flower' *Amorphophallus titanum*, the largest bloom in the world, comes into flower.

Address 1 Brookside, CB2 1JE, +44 (0)1223 336265, www.botanic.cam.ac.uk | Getting there
Bus 26 to Bateman Street | Hours Daily (except public holidays): Apr–Sept 10am–6pm;
Feb, Mar & Oct 10am–5pm; 4pm in the winter | Tip A short walk down Trumpington
Road, past Brooklands Avenue and Newton Road, will bring you to the delightful gates
of St Faith's prep school. Designed in 2006 by sculptor Matthew Lane Sanderson, who
specialises in metalwork using organic and natural themes, the gates conjure up images of
enormous toadstools and twisting branches, and feature four Aladdin-style oil lamps.

17__The Busway

Look! No hands!

Considering the difference in size between the two countries, it's astonishing that the longest guided busway in the world should be in England rather than Australia and what's more, twice the length. But when you take this unique route from the south of Cambridge to St Ives and on to Huntingdon, it's not statistics you're thinking about, it's the revelation that a bus journey can be so exciting.

Take The Busway from start to finish – about 90 minutes – to enjoy the full experience. The bus starts by going through the rapidly expanding medical campus around Addenbrooke's Hospital and the town centre before picking up the main section of the cast concrete guided track just north of the city. From this point driving is hands-free and the buses pick up speed, to a maximum of 56 miles an hour. The suddenness with which you are in open countryside is a striking contrast with the built-up and crowded city streets you have just left. There are frequent stops along the way, where you can get out and explore the villages and conservation areas in this quieter part of Cambridgeshire.

The Busway was first proposed in 2001 as part of a major transport scheme to help relieve congestion on the A14 road and provide an alternative commuter route into the city. Initial reception of the idea was mixed, with the sceptical MP at the time calling it 'a white elephant'. However, the plan went ahead, construction started in 2007 and by 2011 The Busway was in service. Passenger numbers soon exceeded expectations, new stops have since been added and a pedestrian and cycle track runs alongside the entire route.

Whether you are travelling in and out of Cambridge for work, shopping, entertainment or appointments, or taking a car-free day out in St Ives or Huntingdon, the guided bus is a safe, relaxing way to do it without worrying about traffic jams and looking for parking spaces.

Routes, stops, fares and timetables thebusway.info. Tickets are bought from the driver on the bus. | Tip Put on your wellies or walking boots, pick up your binoculars, pack a lunch, and take The Busway to the RSPB reserve at Fen Drayton Lakes. This is a request stop, so tell the driver when you get on that you want to get off there!

18_Caius Court

Unhealthy Cambridge

In June 1348, the plague arrived at a small town on the south coast, and over the next 18 months swept through England. The Black Death is thought to have killed between 25 and 60 per cent of the country's population. Among the wealthy the death toll was minimal, but the crowded, insanitary conditions in which the poor lived made them vulnerable to infection. By the end of 1349, nearly half the country's priests, who worked among the poor, had died. In Cambridge, which had been badly affected by the plague, three colleges were founded at the time, principally to train new clergy. Gonville Hall was one of them.

The Black Death cast a long shadow and for many years afterwards its return was dreaded. And return it did, from time to time. Cambridge was not exempt and was notorious for being an unhealthy place to live: the King's Ditch, built as a defence but in fact an open sewer, ran right through the town. By the early 16th century, Gonville Hall was in serious decline, the victim of inadequate endowments. It was saved by a former student, John Caius, who had been the doctor to three English monarchs (Edward VI, Mary and Elizabeth I). He re-founded the college as Gonville and Caius (usually referred to as Caius) in 1557.

Caius was preoccupied with health. He would not admit students 'suffering from any grave or contagious illness, or an invalid, that is sick in a serious measure'. He extended the college buildings, including a three-sided court, open on one side, 'lest the air from being confined within a narrow space should become foul'. This was a departure from traditional college courts, which were fully enclosed for security and shelter.

John Caius was a pioneer of zoology and anatomy – his college had a grant to receive two corpses a year for dissection. Perhaps predictably, Gonville and Caius developed a reputation for medicine, which it maintains today.

Address Trinity Street, CB2 1TA, +44 (0)1223 332400, www.cai.cam.ac.uk | **Getting there**
Any Citi bus (1–8) to town centre; Grand Arcade car park | **Hours** Check at Porters' Lodge |
Tip John Caius built three gates for his new college. Students enter through Humility, walk
through Virtue on their way around college, and pass through Honour only once, when it is
opened on graduation day. The Gate of Honour is in the open side of Caius Court.

19 Calverley's Brewery

Don't worry, be hoppy

What do a stables, a piggery, an upholsterer, a motor mechanic's, an organ builder's workshop and a micro brewery have in common? The answer is that they have all shared the piece of land that is now 23A Hooper Street – an irregular plot that fronts on to the street with its side running parallel to the railway line.

From 1928 motor mechanic Thomas Fordham occupied 'The Garage', Hooper Street, which continued to be run by the next generation of Fordham family. Their services were greatly appreciated by local residents (as were those of John Reed who carried on after them). And now, equally appreciated by local residents is the garage's successor, the brewery and taproom, opened in 2014 by brothers Sam and Tom Calverley.

Barely visible from Hooper Street (look out for the small hanging sign), Calverley's comprises a clutch of low-rise buildings, one housing the brewery and another the taproom. The taproom is a well-designed bright space, cool and minimal with many a nod to its industrial past, where you will find a hospitable welcome. During the warmer months there is plenty of outdoor seating in the courtyard. In the brewery, they conjure up a mighty range of beers inspired by the constantly evolving beer styles of the world. There's always a new brew to try, with at least a dozen on the menu. Choose from N.E.I.P.A. with notes of grapefruit and pineapple, or an oat stout with just a hint of liquorice and a umami finish, or maybe an easy-drinking lager gently infused with Tettnang and Saaz hops.

But let's just suppose you're not a beer drinker. Happily, there's plenty of choice, from wine, cider and perry to gin and soft drinks. And vegans? Totally catered for. Even your designated driver will be satisfied with the range of alcohol-free choices.

While Calverley's don't provide food, you can order pizzas in from Scott's All Day on Mill Road.

Address 23A Hooper Street, CB1 2NZ, +44 (0)1223 778687, www.calverleys.com | Getting there Citi 2 to Mill Road (Gwydir Street), then a 6-minute walk right to the end of Hooper Street | Hours Tue–Fri 5–10.30pm, Sat noon–10.30pm | Tip Its sister venue, the Engineer's House on Riverside, serves up the same excellent brews but with the added delight of one of the best views in Cambridge. You can enjoy your drinks while watching all the walk, jog, cycle or row right past you.

20__The Cambridge Blue
Top tipples, best beers and winning wines

As in many other towns and cities in Britain, Cambridge's pubs have been dwindling in number since the end of World War II. In recent decades many pubs have been forced to close, due to rising costs and changing social drinking trends. But those that remain are flourishing, and one such pub that has not just survived but gone from strength to strength is The Cambridge Blue.

A fair way from the city centre, halfway down Gwydir Street (it rhymes with 'wider', by the way), The Cambridge Blue nestles in among the Victorian terraced houses of this long, narrow street. As with many Cambridge pubs, there is a long history attached to 'the Blue'. In the 19th century it was opened as the Dewdrop Inn (a terrible Victorian pun), and remained so until 1985 when the new owners, later also the landlords of The Free Press, changed its name to reflect their love of rowing. This seemed curious at the time, as the pub could hardly be much further from the river.

The current owners, Jethro and Terri Littlechild, have made the venue one of the most loved and respected pubs in Cambridge – respected because it must surely have the largest selection of beers not just in Cambridge, but probably in the country. With 226 different bottled beers and a large selection of real ales from the pump, it's no wonder that it has been awarded pub of the year by CAMRA (the Campaign for Real Ale). In addition to this there are over 100 different whiskies to choose from. The food is simple, basic pub grub, at affordable prices.

The Blue's interior is a traditional friendly and cosy space with plenty of interesting pub ephemera on the walls. Outside in the small garden the marquee is an almost permanent fixture, with beer festivals, events, parties and weddings happening much of the time. Right at the end of the garden is a low wall with a unique feature – a helpful step into Mill Road Cemetery.

Address 85–87 Gwydir Street, CB1 2LG, +44 (0)1223 471680, www.cambridge.pub |
Getting there Citi 2 to opposite Gwydir Street | **Hours** Mon–Sat noon–11pm, Sun
noon–10.30pm | **Tip** The Bath House, at the top of Gwydir Street, was opened in 1927 to
provide washing facilities for local people. Many Cambridge residents can still remember
the weekly hot bath, towel and soap for one shilling (5p); the baths closed in 1977 and the
building is now used as a community centre.

21__Cambridge Buddhist Centre

A strange thread linking bawdy comedy to Buddhism

Rather like the railway station, the Festival Theatre was built outside the city boundary, in the area known as Barnwell, to avoid the disapproval of the University, which believed its young charges would be sullied by contact with such a low form of entertainment. Originally known as the Barnwell Theatre, and designed by the architect William Wilkins, it opened in 1814 and is one of only four remaining Georgian theatres outside London. It must have been stunning in its day. Capable of holding up to 900 people, it has a horseshoe auditorium with two tiers of boxes, although the partitions and the seating have long since been removed. By 1878 its fortunes had declined, and it was turned into a mission hall for use by the Evangelisation Society. It had a brief renaissance as a theatre during the 1920s and '30s, reviving during World War II to stage shows for the troops, but then had to close. It became a store for electrical goods, and was finally used for costume storage by the more successful Arts Theatre. Miraculously, it survived being demolished as part of the Grafton Centre development.

The Cambridge Buddhist Centre took over the damp and neglected playhouse in 1998. They have been the most thoughtful tenants possible, preventing any further decline in the fabric of the building, but changing as little as possible in order to retain the theatre's essential character. It is now a thriving centre for classes, discussions and events that include tai chi, yoga, meditation and that current favourite, mindfulness. The sunburst doors at the front open into an attractive, airy Art Deco-style foyer, a 1920s' addition, and everyone is given a genuinely warm welcome by a member of the Centre.

There are now open days when visitors can enjoy a tour of the building, and also occasional concerts and special performances.

Address 38 Newmarket Road, CB5 8DT, +44 (0)1223 577553,
www.cambridgebuddhistcentre.com | **Getting there** Bus 10, 11, 12, 17, 114 or 196 to Napier
Street; Grafton Centre car park | **Hours** Contact the Centre for details of open days, or to
arrange a private or group visit | **Tip** The Friends of Midsummer Common have established
a Community Orchard linking Midsummer Common with the Newmarket Road. It's a
lovely spot where the public can picnic among apple, pear, plum and cherry trees – and
they can pick the fruit when it is ripe. Wild flowers have been planted there for all to enjoy.
Volunteers are always welcome!

22 Cambridge Central Mosque

Europe's first eco-friendly mosque

Approaching the mosque, which is right at the end of the noisy Mill Road, you'll immediately be struck by its beautiful and calm Islamic garden. Visitors can always be found there, including nurses from nearby Brookfields Health Centre taking a well-deserved break.

Right from the start, the planners were keen to involve local residents and ensure their support for the scheme, so that the mosque could be a place for everyone, regardless of their religion. And London Eye architects Marks Barfield really pulled it off.

The concept behind the design was that of a calm oasis within a grove of trees. Its defining feature is its timber structure, using laminated spruce for a series of pillars forming an octagonal canopy that supports the roof. While referencing Islamic design, the structure also evokes the fan vaulting found in King's College Chapel. Dark red bricks spelling out 'Qil huwa Allahu ahad' (God is one) are embedded in traditional Cambridge Gault brickwork. The mosque was formally opened in December 2019 by Turkey's President Erdogan, and in 2021 it was short-listed for the prestigious Stirling Prize for architecture.

The eco-mosque draws on solar power to heat all its water. Stored rainwater and grey water irrigate the garden and flush the toilets. Natural light pours into the entire building, supplemented by low energy LED bulbs. And the excellent insulation and natural ventilation mean that the basement heat pumps generate more energy than they consume.

All areas are shared by men and women up to the point of entry to the prayer hall. Here, movable wood lattice screens enable men and women to pray in the same space (a first for a UK mosque), while there is a gallery on the first floor for women who prefer more privacy.

Do take the time to visit – you will be made to feel most welcome.

Address 309–313 Mill Road, CB1 3DF, +44 (0)1223 654020, www.cambridgecentralmosque.org | Getting there Bus 2 to Madras Road; small underground park at the mosque | Hours Check website before visiting; guided tours (pre-booked through the website) take place on weekend mornings at 11.30am | Tip Cross over Mill Road and have a stroll around the streets of terraced houses. Built between 1880 and 1910, the street names celebrate Empire. Malta, Cyprus, Suez, Madras and Hobart were all ports on the journey to Australia.

23_ Cambridge Cheese Co.

Hello! Is it Brie you're looking for?

Tucked away down a narrow pedestrian-only alleyway just off Bridge Street, and decorated with a profusion of old enamel signs, the Cambridge Cheese Co. is a small, specialist shop that really knows its business and communicates its enthusiasm for fine food to all who venture in there.

Started in 1994 by foodies Jacky and Paul Sutton Adam, the shop soon established a reputation for its knowledge of cheeses of all kinds, carefully selected and then matured in the cool cellar beneath the shop. As business prospered, they expanded to include a line of artisan foods from Britain and Europe that would complement the cheese. Charcuterie and smoked fish sit alongside large bowls of olives and antipasti, jars of pickles and relishes, over 20 sorts of vinegar and many kinds of olive oil. Some like it hot, so for them there is a wide range of over 50 chilli sauces, helpfully arranged beside a copy of the Scoville scale to warn the unwary of the heat units in each kind of chilli. Customers looking for a wine to accompany their purchases can select from a small but well-chosen range supplied by two local independent importers, and niche winemakers Domaine of the Bee.

But the heart of the shop will always lie with the cheese. Camilla Marshall Lovsey is in charge of purchasing and the day-to-day running of the business and is proud of their range of nearly 300 cheeses, many of them seasonal – such as creamy Vacherin Mont d'Or in the winter and tiny production goat's milk cheeses from Provence, like Saint Domnin, in the summer. The selection of British cheeses is large, from the Cambridge made St Ivo to strong, sharp Vintage Lincolnshire Poacher, and their exclusive goat's cheese, Lord Nelson. Their range of European cheeses is also impressive and they even stock Brunost, that decidedly unusual brown fudge-like cheese from Norway. You either love it or you hate it.

Address 4 All Saints' Passage, CB2 3LS, +44 (0)1223 328672, www.cambridgecheese.com |
Getting there Citi 5 to Bridge Street; Grand Arcade car park | **Hours** Mon–Fri
10am–4pm, Sat 10am–5pm | **Tip** All Saints' Garden is a lovely, peaceful place to sit with
a picnic, but it comes alive when local artisans set up their stalls for the Arts and Crafts
Market. This is held every Saturday, and on Wednesday to Saturday throughout December.

24_ Cambridge Junction

Up the Junction, where art meets life

There is a popular local story that when Cambridge Junction was built, it was designed so that if it failed as an arts venue it could quickly be reconfigured as a storage facility. This is a complete myth, according to Ed Hine, the venue's Marketing and PR officer; there was far more optimism than that when the place opened in 1990. Then just a single building, it was created for Cambridge's youth, who had long needed a venue they could call their own. To minimise any noise nuisance, it was deliberately sited away from the centre of the town, far from habitation (no longer the case, with the huge development of housing there has been in the CB1 area) and kicked off with club nights, music, dance, theatre and comedy.

Today, the venue has grown enormously and features J2, a smaller seated space that is perfect for more intimate events, and J3, the experimental and learning space. In many ways, the audience has grown with the space – people who came to the club nights 20 years ago are now returning for gigs, while some are bringing their children to circus and puppet shows. But these are no conventional events; in keeping with the rather edgy surroundings, everything Cambridge Junction puts on is cutting-edge.

Its policy of supporting up-and-coming talent has paid dividends, and Cambridge Junction is seen as a leading venue in the east of England. Some of the best acts going have performed there: Elbow, Radiohead, Amy Winehouse, Mumford and Sons, Tim Minchin, David Mitchell and Eddie Izzard among many others. Other bands and comedians use the place as somewhere to polish their acts prior to a tour – Cambridge audiences are kind and are known for giving performers a chance.

In the words of Rob Tinkler, popular culture manager since 1994, 'A lot of Cambridge Junction's history isn't at the Junction – it's in the hearts and minds of the people of Cambridge.'

Address Clifton Way, CB1 7GX, +44 (0)1223 511511, www.junction.co.uk | Getting there Bus 1A, 3, 13, 13A, 16A or 27 to Hills Road Sixth Form College | Hours See website for event details | Tip Down Purbeck Road, just by the Sixth Form College, is the Scandinavian-style Cambridge Cookery Bistro and Café. Try their cinnamon rolls, artisan breads and cakes, all made on site, or enjoy a light lunch or Sunday brunch. You can also watch bread and croissants being made in the award-winning cookery school next door (www.cambridgecookery.com).

25 The Cambridge Rules
Stay onside and hands off the ball

In 2022 a local news website identified the official rules of football as number one of '20 Amazing Things Cambridge Has Given the World' – ahead of Newton's theory of gravity, Darwin's theory of evolution and Stephen Hawking's black holes, among others. A contentious list but on the other hand the Cambridge Rules were drawn up to end the contention that had bedevilled football as it was played at the University.

Football is supposed to have originated in unruly groups of young men inflating an animal bladder and kicking, throwing or whacking it with sticks through village streets until they exhausted themselves. That may not be far from the truth – similar ball games have been recorded in most cultures since ancient times. However, football now tops the list of the world's most popular team sports that developed from these games, including rugby, hockey and cricket. Like many of these, football was established and legitimised within the privileged environment of British public schools and was very much a gentlemen's game by the mid-19th century.

Not that on-pitch behaviour was gentlemanly. At Cambridge University the widely differing rules that had been determined in these schools led to chaos, as team members played by the conflicting rules of the school they had been to. Something had to be done, and in 1848 a group of 14 men, 12 students and 2 from the town, met in Trinity College to draw up definitive rules for the game. The rules were decided within a few hours and posted on Parker's Piece and still form the basis of the laws of the game today.

Those 14 men could not have imagined the international tournaments, huge wealth, universal appeal and star-making of the modern game when they met to try to civilise their inter-collegiate matches. Appropriately, the monument on Parker's Piece that celebrates their decision records the rules in several languages.

26 Castle Mound

Next stop – the North Pole

In a city as flat as Cambridge, the inhabitants become very excited by hills. Several places with 'hill' in their names are in fact no such thing: the names Peas Hill and Market Hill come from a much older use of the word 'hill', meaning 'meeting place'. So Cambridge's one serious hill is much revered, but beyond its topography, it has a very ancient and surprising history.

If you walk up Castle Street and then climb up Castle Mound, you will be rewarded with one of the best views of the city (and the sight of the cranes everywhere on the horizon will also reveal just how far Cambridge is expanding). Once at the top, some 108 feet above sea level, you might like to try accommodating the thought that there is no higher ground between this point and the North Pole – assuming you were heading straight across East Anglia and out to sea.

Archaeological evidence has shown that the hill's origins go back to Roman times, and that for nearly 1,000 years it was the centre of Cambridge. From the last century B.C. it was in turn a British village, a Roman garrison guarding the river on the road to the north, a fortified Romano-British settlement, a Saxon trading centre, and finally a Norman castle. Each successive generation recognised the strategic advantage of this high point. William the Conqueror visited Cambridge in 1068 on his way back from making peace with King Malcolm of Scotland. To secure his power in the region he had a motte and bailey castle constructed on it, bestriding the old Roman road (motte refers to a raised earthwork – the mound that survives today). Originally of wood, the bailey was rebuilt in stone by Edward I in 1284, but by the 16th century it had fallen into ruins.

On a warm summer's night during May Ball week, which confusingly takes place in June, there's no better place to enjoy the fireworks than on top of Castle Mound.

Address Castle Hill, CB3 0RG | Getting there Citi 5 or 6, Bus 1A or 95 to Castle Street | Hours Accessible 24 hours | Tip The building at the bottom of Castle Mound is Shire Hall, built in 1932 but now closed since the Council relocated. It replaced the site of the castle bailey and the county gaol, and used bricks from the old gaol in its construction.

27 __ Centre for Computing History

From mainframes to microprocessors

Within 50 short years, it's become possible to fit the information that was once stored in a colossal whirring monster the size of an industrial fridge onto something no bigger than a postage stamp. Back then, the only people who had access to these behemoths were white-coated scientists, governments and huge corporations. Today, children take for granted the technology that gives them their mobile phones, tablets and games consoles.

The Centre for Computing History is housed in a huge, cavernous space in what used to be a garage, surrounded by commercial units. In the reception area is a recent donation, an awesome 33-foot by 6.5-foot 'megaprocessor' that is all flashing red lights. Built by Cambridge software engineer James Newman, using the game Tetris as a fun way of showing off the computer's power, it is designed to operate so slowly that people can see how it works.

Walk into the main room and the first things that hit you are the beeps and blips of the computers and arcade game machines, all of which visitors are positively encouraged to try for themselves. You can print your own punch tape and experience life in the 1970s' office, where a black-and-white television plays old news stories. Some disastrous inventions are there, like the C5, Sir Clive Sinclair's electrically assisted three-wheel pedal cycle, alongside *E.T.,* possibly the worst video game of all time (728,000 unsold copies were buried in a landfill site in New Mexico). Mostly, though, it is a story of success and progress, told through thoughtfully written display panels, and fascinating exhibits that include ageing comptometers, mobile phones, Gameboys and calculators, from their very earliest incarnations. Bringing the collection right up to the minute are a 3D printer and a virtual reality game.

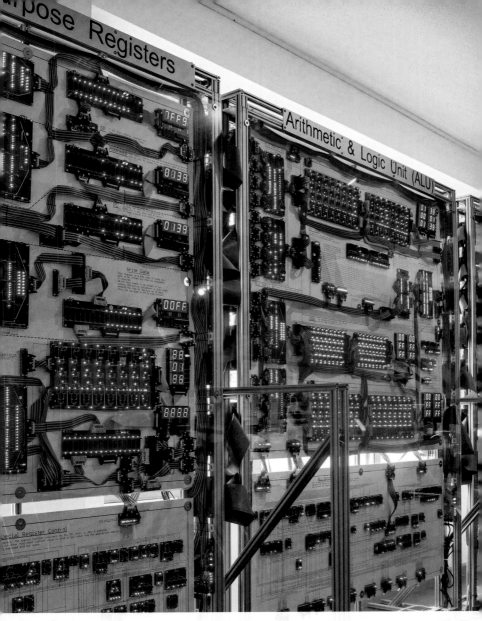

Address Rene Court, Coldhams Road, CB1 3EW, +44 (0)1223 214446, www.computinghistory.org.uk | **Getting there** Bus 17 (every 2 hrs) or Citi 3 to Coldhams Lane; go over the railway bridge and take the very sharp double-back left-hand turn into the estate | **Hours** Wed–Sun 10am–5pm, but daily during school holidays | **Tip** St Barnabas Press, an open-access print workshop, is right next door. For over 30 years it has been running printmaking courses and renting out studios to local artists and tutors.

28 Charles Darwin Sculpture Garden

The gentleman naturalist before he was famous

Aged just 16, Charles Darwin arrived in Edinburgh to study medicine, intending to become a physician. Or rather, his doctor father intended this for him. Charles quickly realised that he could not stand the sight of blood and, worse, was failing in his studies. His long-suffering father then proposed that he should become an Anglican clergyman, an idea Darwin jumped at, as the life of a country parson would allow him to pursue his growing passion for natural history. So it was that in 1827 he arrived in Cambridge to study at Christ's College, but he fared no better this time. His life rapidly descended into a wild round of gambling, drinking, card playing and riding. He ran up large debts, and risked failing his exams and being sent down.

The direction of his life was changed for ever when, neglecting his theological studies, he began to spend time collecting specimens with John Henslow, the Cambridge professor of botany. Henslow recognised his young *protégé*'s skills, curiosity and innate ability; when asked by Captain FitzRoy to suggest a naturalist to join the HMS *Beagle* expedition, he had no hesitation in recommending Darwin.

It is this youthful and high-spirited Darwin, rather than the venerable, bearded Victorian scientist, who is celebrated in the sculpture garden at Christ's College. The sculptor Anthony Smith (a Natural Sciences graduate of Christ's) made use of sketches of Darwin aged 31 to help recreate a likeness of him as a student of 22. Smith spent a year crafting the over-life-sized bronze of the young naturalist lost in thought. He can now be seen perched casually on the end of a bench in the garden, which was specially created to provide a setting for the sculpture. Plants have been chosen to represent stages in Darwin's voyages on HMS *Beagle*.

Address St Andrew's Street, CB2 3BU, +44 (0)1223 334900, www.christs.cam.ac.uk |
Getting there Citi 1, 2, 3, 5, 6 or 8 to opposite Christ's College; Grand Arcade car
park | Hours Daily 9am–4pm, but times may vary; check at Porters' Lodge | Tip Take
a walk down Hobson Street to Sussex Place, home of some of Cambridge's most varied
independent shops. The oldest of these is Millers Music, which has been selling musical
instruments since 1856.

29 __ Cherry Hinton Chalk Pits
The white cliffs of Cambridge

There is something otherwise about the Chalk Pits. When you step through the gate into them, leaving a busy junction behind, you enter an almost alien landscape. Their stillness and scale are disorienting – and you would not be surprised to see Dr Who's TARDIS materialising before your eyes. Then your perspective shifts and you realise you are sharing this extraordinary space with some busy dogs, ambling dog walkers and many hundreds of rabbits.

The Chalk Pits provided material for building in Cambridge and lime for cement, and were quarried until 1980. Even in the winter sun the chalk of the cliffs and bed of the quarry is dazzling; at other times of the year, sunglasses are essential. On an early autumn afternoon, with storm clouds looming in the distance, the Chalk Pits are still a suntrap. The warmth and light accentuate the atmosphere of deep peace, barely disturbed by the sound of the occasional small plane coasting overhead.

A site of special scientific interest, the Chalk Pits are managed as a nature reserve by the Wildlife Trust. Bare chalk areas like these are scarce in the UK. The drought and intense heat that characterise them mean that only hardy plants and organisms thrive here. These include St John's wort, self-heal, fairy flax, a variety of grasses and the very rare moon carrot. These plants will continue to encroach on the rather unforgiving chalk, providing nitrogen for the scant soil covering, until the area becomes grassland. Their seeds provide food for many breeds of small birds and rodents, which in turn provide food for the kestrels that haunt the site.

Next to the Chalk Pit is Limekiln Close, the site of an earlier quarry that was abandoned 200 years ago, which has reverted to its original wild woodland state. This is deeply shaded, with a number of paths and glades, and it provides a striking contrast to the quarry that replaced it.

Address Fulbourn Road, CB1 9JL | Getting there Citi 2 (no car park on the reserve; parking available in residential roads nearby) | Hours Unrestricted | Tip If you cross over the road into the caravan site car park you can explore the old brick kiln. Be prepared to scramble up steep banks over tree roots, to be rewarded with a stunning view from the top.

30__Church of the Holy Sepulchre

Christianity in the round

The Church of the Holy Sepulchre, known as the Round Church, was built in the 12th century, when returning Crusaders wanted a church that reflected the Holy Sepulchre in Jerusalem. Those entering Cambridge by river, and pilgrims to the shrine of Our Lady at Walsingham, stopped there to pray and rest. At that time, the area around Bridge Street was the heart of the town, and for centuries the only crossing point on the river. Cambridge was a major trading centre, with goods coming in from Europe via the east coast. It remained so until the fens were drained in the 17th century and the Cam was no longer navigable.

The Round Church has been extensively altered over time. In the 15th century the Norman windows were replaced with Gothic-style windows, the domed roof was removed and a bell tower erected. The church then suffered from iconoclasm during the Civil War, when most of its painted images were destroyed. It had fallen into disrepair by the 19th century, when it was taken in hand by the highly influential Cambridge Camden Society. This was a body of academics and churchmen who believed in the close association between worship and church design and determined to restore the Round Church, as far as possible, to its original plan. As well as reverting to Norman-style windows, they removed the bell tower and reinstated a domed roof, reminiscent of the original, in its place.

The Victorian stained glass was destroyed by bombing in World War II, but most of the features of the restoration survive, including the floor tiles, which have the arms of Queen Victoria and Prince Albert. Today, the church is an exhibition centre and concert hall. The 'Saints and Scholars' video presentation is an excellent introduction to the town and University.

Address Bridge Street, CB2 1UB, +44 (0)1223 311602, www.roundchurchcambridge.org | Getting there Buses 1, 2, 3, 8 or Citi 5 to Bridge Street; Grand Arcade car park | Hours Tue 1.30–5pm, Wed–Sat 10am–5pm; many different sorts of guided walk start from the church (see website) | Tip The congregation had outgrown the Round Church by the mid-1990s and moved to St Andrew the Great in the centre of town. They have a lot of events and get-togethers, so check their website www.stag.org for details of current activities.

31__Churchill College

Art for education's sake

More than 'just' a University college, Churchill is also the official national and Commonwealth memorial to Sir Winston Churchill. The college holds the entire Churchill archive as well as the papers of more recent prime ministers, including Baroness Thatcher, Sir John Major and Gordon Brown; scientists and inventors, like Frank Whittle and Rosalind Franklin; cabinet ministers; prominent public figures and Nobel Prize winners. The archive rivals the great presidential libraries of the US in terms of invaluable source material on 20th- and 21st-century history.

The spirit of Sir Winston endures in the college, which was founded with an emphasis on science and technology. However, Sir Winston insisted that the arts should also have a place in a fully rounded education. This principle was marked by the start of the sculpture collection featured throughout the college grounds. The collection has both permanent pieces and temporary loans. Among the former is Barbara Hepworth's *Four Square (Walk Through)*. An original Hepworth was in place when the college opened in 1961, on loan and later reclaimed. The students missed it so much that they built a rough replica of it from bricks. When Dame Barbara left *Four Square* to the nation in lieu of death duties it found a place at Churchill, although it remains officially in the collection of the Fitzwilliam Museum.

The sculpture collection is open to the public. Just ask at the Porters' Lodge for entry and a guide. Make sure you do not miss the earliest work in the collection, Geoffrey Clarke's *College Gate*. Now rarely deployed to close the entrance to the college, this handsome and functional piece rests in its open position. Just past the gate, the entrance hall houses an exhibition about the founding of the college that demonstrates how deeply involved Sir Winston was with the development of the college named for him.

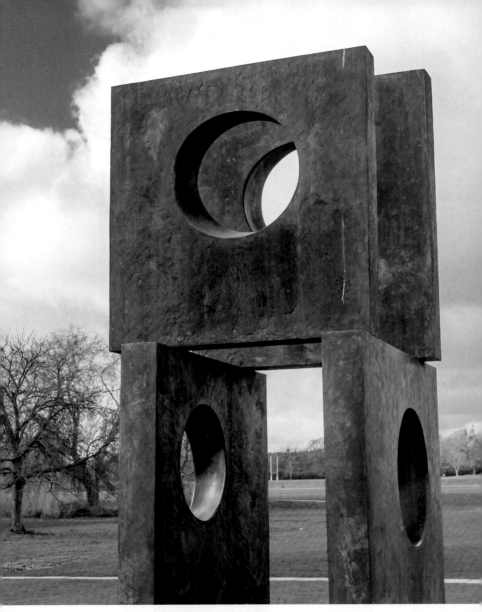

Address Churchill College, Storey's Way, CB3 0DS, +44 (0)1223 366000, www.chu.cam.ac.uk | **Getting there** Bus 3, 8 (not Sun) or Citi 4 (daily) to opposite Storey's Way on Madingley Road | **Hours** As college opening times | **Tip** The building of 'the chapel at Churchill College' led to the resignation of one of the earliest Fellows, Nobel Prize winner Francis Crick, of DNA fame, who was so determinedly against having a religious building in a scientifically oriented college that he sent Sir Winston a cheque for 10 guineas (£10.50) to open a brothel at the college in response. The stained glass is by John Piper.

32__The Clough Gates

Holding out for academic recognition for women

The right for Cambridge University's women students to be awarded degrees was the subject of a long-drawn-out struggle. The time the process took, and several incidents along the way, do not show the University and its members in the best of lights.

Anne Jemima Clough, who is commemorated in the magnificent bronze gates at Newnham College, was a self-educated schoolteacher. In 1871, Henry Sidgwick, a professor who promoted the higher education of women, invited her to take charge of a house in town he had rented for a handful of young women who attended his lectures. Four years later, this establishment settled at Newnham Hall, now known as Old Hall, and Newnham College was founded. At first, Newnham students took courses below degree level, unlike students at Girton, the first women's college, who took the same courses as the men. This caused friction between the two colleges. However, in 1881 women were allowed to sit the same exams as men, and in 1890 a Newnham student outperformed all students in the maths tripos. Recognition of women's success was given grudgingly, in the form of certificates rather than degrees, and in 1897, when a petition for women's right to degrees was rejected, male undergraduates celebrating in the market square caused damage running to thousands of pounds.

When Oxford admitted women to degrees in 1920, things looked hopeful for Cambridge women, but in 1921 the University again rejected their claim. This time, triumphant male students used a coal trolley as a battering ram and attempted to break down the Clough Gates, destroying the lower half. They were faced down by Anne Clough's niece, Thena, a Newnham graduate, who had become Principal of the college the previous year. The University paid for repairs after a fundraising campaign. Cambridge eventually awarded women degrees in 1948 – the last university in the UK to do so.

Address Newnham College, Sidgwick Avenue, CB3 9DF, +44 (0)1223 335700, www.newn.cam.ac.uk | Getting there Bus 199 to Grange Road | Hours College grounds normally open to the public; contact Porters' Lodge to check | Tip In Newnham Walk look up to see the Unequal-Hours Sundial, a memorial to Margaret Stanier who was a Fellow of Newnham College and avid designer of sundials. She was also an enthusiastic bell-ringer, which is acknowledged by the small bell supporting the sundial's gnomon.

33_ The Cook Memorial

'He left nothing unattempted'

Captain James Cook (1728–79) was one of the greatest British naval explorers, whose voyages of discovery were once as well known to British schoolchildren as those of Drake, Raleigh, Livingstone and Scott. He charted the Atlantic coast of Newfoundland and opened up the South Pacific Ocean, discovering and mapping unknown lands, including Australia, Tahiti, New Zealand and Hawaii. Hawaii is where he died, following a disastrous breakdown in relations with the indigenous inhabitants. The story that he was eaten, at least in part, by his killers is probably true: their cannibalism was well known. His bones were returned to his ship and Cook was buried at sea.

In St Andrew the Great there is a memorial that bears his name but principally commemorates his children and his wife, Elizabeth, who lived to the extraordinary age of 93 at a time when the average life expectancy was 40 – and even less for women of childbearing age. James and Elizabeth Cook had a daughter and five sons, not an unusually large 18th-century family, but perhaps remarkable in view of the fact that during their 17-year marriage they spent only four years together. The memorial reveals the saddest of family stories. Elizabeth not only survived her husband by 56 years but also outlived all her children. Her sons Hugh, a student at Christ's College, and James are buried with her in the church. None had children of their own, so the memorial records the finite history of an entire family.

Contemporaries noted that Elizabeth suffered dreadfully from these losses and was bedridden with grief for two years. At the end of her long life she left funds to maintain this memorial and pay for the care of five elderly women in the parish. Years later, Elizabeth's bequest stopped the church being turned into the Cambridge tourist information office and it is now the centre of a thriving congregation.

IN MEMORY

of *CAPTAIN* JAMES COOK, of the ROYAL NAVY, one of the moſt celebrated Navigators, that this, or former Ages can boaſt of; who was killed by the Natives of *Owyhee*, in the *Pacific Ocean*, on the 14th Day of February, 1779; in the 51ſt Year of his Age.

Of Mr. NATHANIEL COOK, who was loſt with the *Thunderer* Man of War, Captain *Boyle Walſingham*, in a moſt dreadful Hurricane, in October, 1780; aged 16 Years.

Of Mr. HUGH COOK, of *Chriſt's College*, CAMBRIDGE, who died on the 21ſt of December, 1793; aged 17 Years.

Of JAMES COOK, Eſq; COMMANDER in the ROYAL NAVY, who loſt his Life on the 25th of January, 1794; in going from *Pool*, to the *Spitfire* Sloop of War, which he commanded; in the 31ſt Year of his Age.

Of ELIZ^th COOK, who died April 9th 1771, Aged 4 Years.
JOSEPH COOK, who died Septr 13th 1768, Aged 1 Month.
GEORGE COOK, who died Octr 1ſt 1772, Aged 4 Months.

All Children of the firſt mentioned CAP^t JAMES COOK by ELIZABETH COOK, who survived her Husband 56 Years, & departed this life 13th May 1835, at her residence Clapham Surrey in the 94th Year of her Age. Her remains are deposited with those of her Sons JAMES & HUGH, in the middle Aisle of this Church.

Address St Andrew the Great, St Andrew's Street, CB2 3AX | Getting there Citi 2 to St Andrew's Street; Grand Arcade car park | Hours Sundays and by appointment (churchoffice@stag.org; +44 (0)1223 518218) | Tip Cross the road and walk up Christ's Lane and you'll reach Christ's Pieces, an attractive open space with a rather Victorian feel, that provides a little peace and calm in this otherwise noisy and bustling part of town. The small Princess Diana Memorial Garden on the north-west corner of the park offers a welcome place to rest.

34__ The Corpus Clock

Time is not on your side

In 2008, *Time* magazine listed John C. Taylor's Chronophage, or Time Eater, as one the best inventions of the year. But is the Corpus Clock a machine, or a work of art, or both?

In the space of a very few years, the clock has become one of Cambridge's most famous and visited sights. Opposite King's College and occupying what was once the front entrance to a bank, the clock dominates the view down King's Parade. The Time Eater itself is a huge and malevolent grasshopper that turns the timepiece, swallowing the seconds as it does so. The symbolism is confirmed in the Latin inscription underneath, which means 'The world is passing away, along with its desires'.

This reminder of the transience of things has nevertheless been built to last, with the main components made from stainless steel and gold. The clock mechanism itself is turned inside out: the usually small part that makes the gears move is known as a grasshopper escapement. The Corpus Clock has made this part the principal feature and wittily dramatised the function.

The outer ring on the clock shows the seconds, the middle ring the minutes, and the inner ring the hours, lit by a race of blue LED lights. Strictly speaking, the clock is only accurate once every five minutes, but then it is accurate to one hundredth of a second. Try if you can to view the clock on the hour, when the show of lights is most spectacular and the grasshopper unnervingly gulps down another hour you will never see again.

John C. Taylor is an inventor and philanthropist who gave the Chronophage to his old college as part of a larger donation that converted the former bank to a college library. 'Conventional clocks with hands are boring,' he said. 'I wanted to make timekeeping interesting.' The clock was unveiled, appropriately, by Professor Stephen Hawking, the author of the bestselling *A Brief History of Time*.

Address Corpus Christi College, Trumpington Street, CB2 1RH | Getting there Bus 199 to opposite Corpus Christi; Grand Arcade car park | Hours Accessible 24 hours; college hours 10.30am – 4.30pm, July – Sept | Tip Directly opposite the Corpus Clock on the Keyes Building at King's College is a blue plaque honouring Alan Turing, mathematician, codebreaker, and innovator in computer science and artificial intelligence.

35 Cromwell's Head

Protecting the Protector

In 1960, the Master of Sidney Sussex College was offered a macabre gift – the mummified head of Sidney's most famous old boy, Oliver Cromwell, who led the anti-royalist Roundheads in the English Civil War and ruled the nation as Lord Protector of the Commonwealth for five years. Cromwell was not a great student and left without taking a degree, but his return to Sidney four centuries later marked the end of a long and very strange journey. After the restitution of the monarchy in 1660, Cromwell's body was dug up and symbolically executed. His head was displayed on a pole outside Westminster for more than 20 years, then exhibited widely until the early 19th century. Eventually the head was inherited by a clergyman who returned it discreetly to Sidney. After forensic tests proved that it was indeed the head of Cromwell, it was buried near the college chapel. Because of threats from pro-royalist sympathisers, the precise location is a secret passed on from Master to Master by word of mouth. A plaque in the chapel records the event.

Founded in 1596, Sidney is the youngest of the 'old' University colleges, and for over 200 years it was the newest in Cambridge. While it lacks the flamboyance and space of some of the grander foundations, Sidney has been quietly successful in academic and public life, and always open to change. It was one of the first 'old' colleges to admit women, and the first of the previously all-male colleges to appoint a female Master.

The college buildings are architecturally modest and Sidney's position means it's often called 'the one opposite Sainsbury's'. But Sidney is a pocket of calm that preserves the atmosphere of the Franciscan friary that originally stood on its site. The wisteria that climbs the college walls is a burst of colour in the spring and transforms Sidney Street during the winter months, when it is threaded with lights.

Address Sidney Street, CB2 3HU, +44 (0)1223 338800, www.sid.cam.ac.uk | Getting there Citi 1, 2, 3, 5, 6 or 8 to Hobson Street, or Red Park & Ride; Grand Arcade car park | Hours Variable; contact Porters' Lodge to check | Tip Don't miss the striking blue and silver porcupine, the symbol of the Sidney family, on the walkway above Sussex Street.

36__David Parr House

A small artistic miracle

The craftsman-painter David Parr, a boy from a working-class family, was apprenticed at an early age to Frederick Leach and Co., the decorative arts company whose workshops were in City Road, Cambridge. Leach and his workshop were responsible for the outstanding Arts and Crafts decoration inside many of Cambridge's colleges and neo-Gothic churches, including All Saints', St Botolph's, and the ceiling of the Old Hall in Queens' College.

Parr clearly prospered, and by 1887 was able to buy a small house in Gwydir Street; over the next 40 years, when he had the time and the materials, he embellished every room in the house with astonishing painting, stencilling and lettering that mirrored the work he was carrying out in far grander buildings. At his death in 1927 his granddaughter Elsie, then aged 12, came to live here with her grandmother, and remained for the next 85 years. During that time she married Alfred Palmer, who worked on the railways, and raised two daughters. It was her sense of the importance of her grandfather's work that kept the interior of the house almost completely unchanged during that time. It couldn't have been easy for any of them, as the house is very simple and quite lacking in modern comforts, but in many ways it is thanks to Elsie's frugality that everything has been so well preserved.

Entering the house today is a magical experience – it is almost as if Elsie has just stepped outside for a moment. Her coat and umbrella are still in the hall; Alfred's British Railways uniform hangs in an upstairs wardrobe and there are reminders of her life in every drawer and cupboard.

The house was unknown to all but a handful of family members until 2013, when historian Tamsin Wimhurst chanced upon it and arranged for it to be bought by a trust, to ensure that this remarkable time capsule could be kept and enjoyed by future generations.

Address 186 Gwydir Street, CB1 2LW, www.davidparrhouse.org | **Getting there** Citi 2 to Mill Road, near Gwydir Street | **Hours** Thu – Sat, timed visits of 1 hour 30 minutes at 9.30am, 11.30am, 1.30pm & 3.30pm. Booking essential; visit www.davidparrhouse.org to check availability | **Tip** Dale's Brewery opposite dates from 1903 and is now home to two shops selling antiques and bric-à-brac, and the café Hot Numbers, which arguably serves the best cup of coffee in Cambridge.

37 __ Dinky Doors

Wonder as you wander

At a time of almost constant bleak news, it's reassuring to know that someone out there is on a mission to Save the World. By making tiny doors. What?

The Dinky Doors team of Dinky and Doorky made their first tiny door out of tin foil and polymer clay. It was attached to the front of Roll On Blank Tapes in Gwydir Street, which shut its own doors in 2002 and remained untouched until put up for sale recently. The door vanished almost at once – to adorn some student bedroom perhaps? The lesson was learned. All the installations since then have been made of steel and welded in place.

The joy of these miniature sculptures is coming across them by accident, as they're tucked away at ground level and need a keen eye to spot them. You may spy the Wonder Emporium in Sussex Place, a quirky collection of objects found by the creators, all of which are for sale at 3p apiece. The Museum of Zoology and Downing Street have mingled together to produce a familiar black door, number 10 1/4, where the inhabitant seems to have purple tentacles. A recent challenge was the doorway in All Saints' Passage that reveals how polar opposites, Mr D. Mon and Angela, met and fell in love. By some terrible mischance, Dinky Doors' Supreme Leader's perilous visit to Earth to check on the progress of tiny door installation ended in disaster when he crashed into the walls of the Museum of Technology. A trail of footprints hint at the fact that he is now living somewhere in the museum, where you may be lucky enough to come across him. An early creation, attached to Reality Checkpoint (see ch. 90), advises people to 'check reality yourself'. Something we all need to do in these strange times.

Are there more Dinky Doors to come (they're currently up to 15)? While the team remain characteristically enigmatic, they're always thinking of new doors of hope to happier worlds. Recent additions have been Mage's Pages and Dinky Shrinky.

Address Their website www.dinkydoors.co.uk gives the locations of all the places where these tiny sculptures can be spotted | **Getting there** Most Dinky Doors are in, or close to, the town centre, and can be easily reached on foot. The furthest out can be spotted at Wandlebury, a short car or bus ride (Stagecoach 13, 13A, 13B or 613) from town | **Tip** For street art on a somewhat grander scale, www.cambridgesculpturetrails.co.uk takes you on three walking trails past all of Cambridge's pieces of sculpture, and explains the story behind each one.

38 The Eagle

Beer and the secret of life

In the very heart of Cambridge, just a stone's throw from the world-famous King's College, lies The Eagle public house. It is not only one of the oldest pubs in the city but the only remaining coaching inn that in any way resembles its original form, with a large courtyard for the departing coaches. Owned by Corpus Christi College, but managed by brewers Greene King, The Eagle – originally The Eagle and Child – has been a popular and well-frequented pub since the 1600s. During the 18th century and until the advent of the railways, The Eagle was a busy centre of travel, helping to transport people to destinations all over the country.

In all its long history perhaps its most famous and best-known era was the middle of the 20th century. What is still known as the Airmen's Bar was used by British and American pilots during World War II, when the now famous ceiling was covered with graffiti by the airmen. This they did with candles and cigarette lighters, and there is even a rendering of a naked woman done in lipstick (thought to be Ethel, sister of the landlord). Not long after the war, the pub became a regular haunt of Francis Crick and James Watson. An excited Crick rushed in one lunchtime from the Cavendish Laboratory where they worked to announce that he and Watson had 'discovered the secret of life' in the form of the structure of DNA.

In 1988 the pub closed its doors with an uncertain future ahead, but in 1992 it reopened after extensive renovation. The deteriorating ceiling was restored, and new bars opening directly on Bene't Street were created. These were painstakingly constructed to look ancient, and most visitors assume that they are as old as the rest of the building (they were in fact part of an estate agent's premises). Pine panelling dating from the 18th century has been carefully restored.

And, as you might expect, it has its own ghost, the victim of a fire. A window is always kept open for it on an upper floor.

Address 8 Bene't Street, CB2 3QN, +44 (0)1223 505020, www.eagle-cambridge.co.uk | Getting there Bus 199 to opposite Bene't Street; Grand Arcade car park | Hours Mon–Wed 11am–11pm, Thu–Sat 11am–midnight, Sun 11am–10.30pm | Tip Cross over to Free School Lane. The tiny patch of ground on the left is all that remains of the original Botanic Garden, established in 1762 as a physic garden (devoted to the growing of medicinal plants).

39 __ Eddington

An inspirational, aspirational new community

Eddington is the jewel in the crown of Cambridge city development. Ten years in the planning, the award-winning new community proves that time spent on planning is never wasted, a rule many thought had been negated by the unpopular development to the south of the city.

Eddington is the result of a partnership between the city and the University, which shared a need for affordable housing for residents, staff and students. They envisioned a sustainable new community in which learning and working would thrive, incorporating a state-of-the-art infrastructure for energy, communications, water and waste. The first homes were finished in 2019, and the first stage of the development has been completed with a community centre, school, supermarkets and recreational spaces.

How do you choose a name for a new area? Its proximity to the Institute of Astronomy was an obvious source of ideas. Sir Arthur Eddington was a physicist who vindicated Einstein's Theory of Relativity. Road names commemorate local figures and Cambridge academics, including Martin Ryle, Edward Storey, Bertha Swirles, Alan Turing and Margaret Wileman.

Affordable housing means economical and practical design – inevitably blocks of flats (there will be larger properties in due course). The developers chose several designers to produce a variety of plans, all to the same brief, resulting in different façades and materials and environmentally sensitive features. Some of these are clearly visible – like the bat and bird roosts on the buildings – while others are hidden. You won't see wheelie bins on Eddington pavements, while the lake is just one part of the largest water recycling system in the UK.

Connectivity is as important as sustainability for this extension to the city. Eddington is within easy distance of the city centre and its lake and green spaces make it a popular destination for weekend walkers.

Address CB3 1AA | Getting there Free parking at Madingley Road P&R; bus route U from Cambridge Station | Tip Storey's Field Centre, Eddington's community space, was shortlisted for the 2018 RIBA Stirling Prize and has won regional RIBA awards for outstanding design, sustainability and building of the year. It hosts a number of cultural events for Eddington and city residents.

40_ Efes Restaurant

A proper Turkish delight

If you'd been living in Cambridge in the late 1980s and early '90s, you might well have found your way to Mr Chips. But by 1993 it was time for Mr Chips to say goodbye, and this provided the opportunity for Emin Refioglu to open the Turkish restaurant that is still there and thriving over 30 years on.

This small, cosy eatery takes pride in having provided the same offering since it opened: delicious, simply cooked Turkish food and great customer service. Why change things when this is clearly what people want? Efes is always full to bursting and everyone leaves with a contented smile on their face. People don't visit Efes for a quiet, intimate dining experience. There's always a loud buzz of conversation, and tables and chairs are packed in closely, so you're quite likely to get talking to the people next to you.

What you see is what you get, which is to say that much of the food is laid out in front of you, ready to be cooked on the charcoal grill. The meat and fish are sourced from London, while everything else is bought locally – all of which guarantees freshness and quality, the key to Efes' food offering. Chef Yasar Arslan has been behind the grill almost since Efes opened, continues to cook all the meat and fish himself, and manages to look cool and cheerful despite the blistering heat. These days his son-in-law helps out in the kitchen, prepping all the food.

But don't imagine that Efes is nothing but a meatfest. Vegetables, rice and bread are also key players in any Turkish meal, and the choice of dishes is considerable. Most popular dishes? The mixed kebab and the yogurt chicken that have been on the menu right from the start. The hungriest customers order the set menu, which moves from starters through mains to baklava, but beware – it's a huge amount of food (and very popular with meat-starved students home for the holidays).

Address 80 King Street, CB1 1LD, +44 (0)1223 500005, www.efes-cambridge.co.uk |
Getting there Bus 8 or 8A to Jesus Lane | Hours Mon–Fri noon–2.30pm, 6–11pm, Sat &
Sun noon–11pm | Tip Start or finish your evening off with a visit to The Champion of the
Thames ('The Champ' to its friends), a tiny jewel of a pub serving traditional ales and more.
Or come with some friends and try the Tuesday night quiz.

41 Emma's Duck Pond

Getting the bird

Emmanuel College (Emma to its friends) somehow manages to be off the beaten track and right in the centre of the city at the same time. While not benefiting from the obvious charm of a riverside position, the college more than compensates for this with the sheer magnificence of its buildings. Founded in 1584 with the purpose of training endless numbers of educated clergy for the reformed church, Emma was once the largest Cambridge college. This is no longer the case, but there is one thing that Emma has that no other college can boast of, and that's the ducks. What's more, the ducks are fabled to be the reincarnated souls of former Fellows. To reach the duck pond, visitors will need to march past the front court and through the cloisters – a difficult and frustrating thing to do, since both are worth lingering over. But they can always be visited on the return journey, along with the magnificent chapel, an early work by Sir Christopher Wren.

The pond in the paddock is on the site of the fishpond that was once part of the original friary. Although stocked with some exotic species of duck, such as mandarins, it's hard persuading them to stay there, so what the visitor will most likely encounter is a mixture of mallards and domestic white ducks. These friendly creatures seem to prefer spending their time with the many moorhens that also call Emma home, pecking at the grass and looking expectantly at visitors resting on the benches, in the hope of being thrown a few crumbs.

The adjacent Fellows' Garden, which is unfortunately not open to the public, contains a swimming pool that is perhaps the oldest still in use in the country. Although the water is now crystal clear, within living memory it was so green with algae that a college Fellow who liked to swim lengths along the bottom complained that he lost his way. A line was painted to help him navigate.

Address St Andrew's Street, CB2 3AP, +44 (0)1223 334200, www.emma.cam.ac.uk |
Getting there Citi 1, 3, 7 or 8 to Emmanuel Street; Grand Arcade car park | **Hours** Daily
9am–5pm, but closed during exam periods | **Tip** Cross the road and indulge in some retail
therapy or a coffee in the Grand Arcade.

42 Fitzbillies

Possibly the stickiest buns in the world

Generations of residents, students and visitors have made a beeline for Fitzbillies in search of just one thing – the legendary and peerless Chelsea bun. Unlike any other buns going by the same name, in Cambridge or anywhere else, Fitzbillies' buns have a stickiness and depth that are unmatched. In fact, they are so good that they are exported to seven continents, including Antarctica. Unsurprisingly, the recipe is a secret known only to the head baker.

The cake shop has been a Cambridge institution since 1922 and has weathered a number of crises, including a fire in 1998 that closed the shop for almost a year. Worse, in 2011 it became a victim of the recession and Cambridge city's sky-high rents, with bailiffs arriving to eject customers and staff from the premises. Yet it was at this worst point in its history that its fortunes changed. The actor Stephen Fry bewailed the fate of Fitzbillies on X, formerly Twitter – a tweet seen by his many thousands of followers. Among them were Tim Hayward and Alison Wright, a couple with nerves of steel, and a vision that the business could not only survive but also grow into something even bigger and better. On the day Fitzbillies was back in business, people began queuing long before the doors opened.

Now the beautiful Art Deco window of the original shop shows off a seductive display of cakes, pastries, cupcakes, chocolates and – of course – the legendary buns. The light airy space inside now serves as cake shop, coffee counter and café, and is open throughout the day, seven days a week, for everything from cooked breakfast, coffee, lunch and afternoon tea to the almost equally sought-after Chelsea bun ice cream.

Fitzbillies doesn't take bookings, so you will have to take your chance for a table in this popular café. But don't worry: a second Fitzbillies, serving a selection of sandwiches and salads, and fresh bread can be found on Bridge Street, and a third shop on King's Parade.

Address 52 Trumpington Street, CB2 1RG, +44 (0)1223 352500, www.fitzbillies.com; 36 Bridge Street, CB2 1UW | Getting there Bus 199 to opposite Corpus Christi; Grand Arcade car park | Hours Mon–Fri 8am–6pm, Sat & Sun 9am–6pm | Tip After buying your buns, stroll down Silver Street for a perfect view of the river and a pint at The Anchor, where you will also be able to wash your sticky fingers.

43_ The Fitzwilliam Museum

A wonderful place to hang out

For a traditional arts and antiquities museum that has been ranked alongside London's British Museum, the Fitz (as it is affectionately known) often attracts an unlikely degree of media interest, from spectacular accidents that destroyed exhibits, and sophisticated thefts amounting to £ millions, to controversy over a new rehanging programme.

In 2024, curators abandoned classic chronological hanging and five of the galleries were reorganised along themes – identity, migration and movement, nature, men looking at women, and interiors. The labelling was rewritten to emphasise the intention to practise inclusivity and encourage a new eye on the exhibits. While art commentators questioned whether the museum had been entirely successful in achieving this, the Fitz found it had laid itself open to wider charges of 'wokeness'. But anything that draws people's attention to a museum is good and there is a huge amount in the Fitz's collections and exhibitions to see and learn about – from the ancient world to the present day – however arranged.

The museum moved to its current, purpose-built site in 1848, having occupied various buildings after it was founded in 1816, the legacy of Viscount FitzWilliam, after whom it is named. Further galleries and exhibition spaces have been added to house the diverse collections, including ceramics (there are some intriguing and comical gems here), manuscripts, coins, and of course paintings, among which are masterpieces of British and European art, from Titian to Matisse – and everyone in between. Children love the Egyptian exhibits (yes, there is a mummy) and the room full of armour. Entry is free (although donations are encouraged) so you can take a break from shopping to drop in to look at a specific object or painting. Alternatively, the excellent café and shop could encourage you to pace yourself and make a day of it.

Address 32 Trumpington Street, CB2 1RB, +44 (0)1223 332900, www.fitzmuseum.cam.ac.uk |
Getting there Any Citi bus (1–8) to the town centre; Grand Arcade or Queen Anne Terrace
car parks | **Hours** Tue–Sat 10am–5pm, Sun and Bank Holiday Mon noon–5pm | **Tip**
Across the road from the museum you will see the multi-column, colourful façade of Judge
Business School, one of the leading schools of management in the UK and part of the
University. The school occupies the building that used to be known as Old Addenbrooke's
hospital; the former Outpatients' Department is now the popular Browns restaurant.

44_Flower Trail

Daisies with a difference

It's easy to become fixated on what is immediately in front of you, but if you look up above Cambridge's shops and pubs, with their modern and often unsightly façades, you'll spot a wealth of attractive features – coats of arms, gargoyles, lamps, ornate carvings and commemorative plaques. However, there is one place where it actually pays to look down.

Starting outside St John's College in Bridge Street and carrying on to Magdalene College are 600 brass flowers set into the paving slabs. There is nothing to tell the passer-by what these objects are, and people have speculated whether they might be something to do with pavement safety, or a measurement of distance. Installed in 2001, the flowers were initially something of a trip hazard, but with the passing of time they have been comfortably worn down.

They are in fact a public artwork by sculptor Michael Fairfax, who took as his inspiration the marguerite, the insignia of Lady Margaret Beaufort, founder of St John's, and also the symbol of St Mary Magdalene. The intention was to encourage pedestrians to follow the trail up the road, across the bridge and beyond, with the flowers forming a straight line leading up to a large piece of sculpture at the Castle Hill end of the street. The street-side bollards that run alongside are by the same artist.

The 11.5-foot bronze at the top, called 'Cambridge Core', was not the artist's original design, but came about after workers excavating for Anglian Water's new sewers came across a hoard of 1,800 medieval gold and silver coins, each with a face value of £10 (now preserved in the Fitzwilliam Museum). Archaeologists were brought in to check the excavation before pipes were laid, and drew images illustrating every half-metre of time. Once Michael Fairfax learned of this, he interpreted these drawings onto the core, making his work a history lesson of the site.

Address Bridge Street, CB2 1UF (44a) to (44b) | Getting there Buses 1, 2, 3, 8 or Citi 5 to Bridge Street; Grand Arcade car park | Tip Once known as Desolation Row because of the number of empty shops, Bridge Street now houses some of the city's most elegant, and expensive, independent retailers.

45 foodPark and Food Trucks

Real food, not fast food

The concept of food trucks is not new to the streets of Cambridge – vans selling food to late-night drinkers on their way home are a familiar sight all over the city – but recent years have seen an extraordinary explosion in street food from around the world. This is genuinely good food that uses carefully sourced ingredients full of big flavours, served quickly and cheaply and made (mostly) to be eaten on the move.

From the traders' perspective, their overheads are far lower than for a restaurant, with the big advantage of being able to move to a new location if business is slow. For the customer, it means a choice of well-made, innovative food that can be eaten at any time of the day and well into the night.

The community that has sprung up around the railway station has brought with it the need for shops, bars and places to eat, and the collective of street food traders known as the foodPark has really put street food on the map. An amazing array of colourful old trucks and vans provide the mobile kitchens from which food of all kinds is served – from authentic thin and crispy wood-fired pizzas and truly amazing burgers to Asian delights, *rösti* and ice cream. And there's plenty of choice for vegetarians. More recent venues in west Cambridge, the Science Park and the Cambridge Biomedical Campus now cater for the needs of working communities at these sites. A new development is a lunch market each Friday from noon to 2pm at Eddington, the growing community in north west Cambridge.

Some of Cambridge's newest and most popular venues have recognised the benefits that the food trucks can bring and welcome them on different nights. Social media has meant that you can go on to your favourite food providers' websites or Facebook pages and track them down on any given day of the week. Just buy your food, get a drink and then settle down at one of the tables to enjoy it.

Address (45a) West CB3 0FS, (45b) Science Park CB4 0FN, (45c) CB1 Mill Park, off Station Road, (45d) Eddington CB3 1SE, (45e) Cambridge Biomedical Campus, www.foodparkcam.com | *Getting there* Check website for locations | *Hours* See website | *Tip* If you are visiting the station foodPark, it is worth taking a proper look at the station building itself. Built in 1845, far out of the city centre at the University's insistence, to deter students from being tempted by the fleshpots of London, it is decorated all around its façade with the shields of Cambridge colleges.

46 The Fort St George

An ancient connection to the Indian subcontinent

Of all the many riverside pubs in Cambridge, the Fort St George in England, to give it its full title, is arguably the most attractive and its location is stunning by any standards. Set right on the river opposite several college boathouses, there is a courtyard garden where you can sit and watch the rowing crews train for the Bumps and of course the world-famous boat race on the Thames at London. On the other side of the building there is another garden that overlooks the expansive Midsummer Common. Whichever side you sit on, you could be forgiven for thinking that you were in a far more rural setting than a city centre.

Many years ago, the long, low, timber-framed building (constructed from timbers once used in boats) was situated on an island that had a lock and a ferry to convey people to and fro. The pub derives its name from a fort on an island in the Indian city of Madras. Although the Cambridge 'fort' is on nothing like the same scale, a traveller returning from the subcontinent was taken by the similarity of the islands and so the pub acquired its name, which has endured over three centuries.

The interior is every bit as charming as the exterior. The panelled snug by the main entrance has attractive ancient beams and some intriguing old prints. In the dining area an inglenook fireplace was discovered, having previously been covered by a Victorian one, but the pub's best feature is the huge plate-glass window, right on the riverside, where you can watch the houseboats chug slowly by – a contrast to the rowing eights that streak past at considerable speed.

No wonder, then, that the Prince and Princess of Wales, then the Duke and Duchess of Cambridge, chose the Fort for a quiet lunch on a visit to the city in 2012. The pub has commemorated this by reserving a table for their first child, Prince George, with a plaque that reads 'Reserved for HRH The Prince of Cambridge'.

Address Midsummer Common, CB4 1HA, +44 (0)1223 354327, www.fortstgeorge-cambridge.co.uk | Getting there Bus 95 or Citi 4 to Chesterton Road / Victoria Avenue | Hours Mon – Sat noon – 11pm, Sun noon – 10.30pm | Tip For those with deep pockets, the two-Michelin-starred Midsummer House restaurant next door, housed in an elegant Victorian villa, offers a unique dining experience. Reservations essential.

47__The Free Press

What the papers said

There are three pubs within just a few yards of one another tucked away in a quiet residential area behind the police and fire stations on Parker's Piece. Space is not generous in The Free Press, but what it lacks in size it more than makes up for in character and charm, as well as fine cask ale and food that's well above the usual pub offering.

In the early 19th century, just as a temperance newspaper called the *Free Press* was launched to campaign against the evils of drinking alcohol, a local woman opened up her house to sell her home-brewed ale. The paper lasted for just one issue but the name remained, perhaps kept by the brewer as an ironic reminder of whose offering was the more popular.

During the 1980s, the pub narrowly escaped demolition to make way for the huge modern shopping mall known as the Grafton Centre. This new development was unpopular with many at the time, but the fight to save the district known as the Kite ultimately failed, and a large number of old houses and shops were demolished. Happily for The Free Press, the location of the Grafton development was moved and the pub survived.

Previous landlords were rowing enthusiasts, and their legacy survives in the form of half a boat hanging from the ceiling. It was on its way to the starting line for the annual boat race but crashed into a barge. On it, the embarrassed cox has written 'All my own work'. Today, the décor reflects more the pub's literary link. The ceiling of the snug (tiny, at no more than 5 feet by 4 feet, but once crammed with no fewer than 59 Downing College students) is covered with newspapers, the oldest dating back to 1915. Six letterpress trays on the main bar walls contain an eclectic collection of small objects left by customers, from photographs to train tickets and even a letter to 'the beautiful blue-eyed blonde' spotted in the pub by a love-struck customer. It's not known if they ever got together.

Address 7 Prospect Row, CB1 1DU, +44 (0)1223 368337, www.freepresscambridge.com | **Getting there** Any bus to Drummer Street Bus Station; Queen Anne Terrace car park | **Hours** Tue–Sat noon–11pm, Sun noon–9pm, although kitchen hours are more restricted | **Tip** A short walk across Eden Street and Clarendon Street will bring you to Orchard Street. The row of picturesque bungalow-style cottages on the north side was built in 1825 by Charles Humfrey, an architect and one-time mayor of Cambridge, probably for his own servants.

48 _ G. David Bookseller

Conspicuously inconspicuous since 1896

The 1926 lithograph of Gustave David by Sir William Nicholson hanging above the basement stairs shows a portly, slightly rumpled elderly man wrapped in a large overcoat, cigarette in mouth, a homburg pulled down low on his head, and sporting a rather natty pair of spats. He sits on a crate by his bookstall on Cambridge market, and beside him a gowned student riffles through his stock.

David was born in Paris in 1860, but moved to London and then to Cambridge, where he started his market stall in 1896. The stall carried on after his death 40 years later (until 1981) but he also opened a bookshop in St Edward's Passage – still going today and where his great-grandson David Asplin is one of three partners. It was said of David that 'he awarded his books rather than sold them', but despite his eccentricities his role in the intellectual life of Cambridge was recognised by the University towards the end of his life, when they offered him either an honorary MA or a lunch in Trinity College: he chose the lunch.

Cambridge used to be full of bookshops, but now most of these are gone and David's is the only one of the long-established shops still trading independently. It remains steadfastly old-fashioned, with a minimal presence on the internet and no online trading. Instead, it relies on customers visiting so that the staff can pass on their encyclopaedic knowledge of the shop's stock. Every corridor and room is stacked from floor to ceiling with second-hand and remaindered books: novels, poetry and a huge range of non-fiction that spans architecture to zoology. In the imposing antiquarian room, first editions of *Winnie the Pooh*, *Alice in Wonderland*, James Bond novels and Darwin's *On the Origin of Species* sit comfortably alongside illuminated manuscript leaves from the 1480s, early printed books that go back to the 16th century and huge drawers full of fascinating prints.

Address 16 St Edward's Passage, CB2 3PJ, +44 (0)1223 354619, www.gdavidbookseller.com | Getting there Any Citi bus (1–8) to town centre; Grand Arcade car park | Hours Tue–Sat 10am–4pm | Tip Just opposite are two tiny treasures: the cosy Indigo Coffee House, where six people constitute a crowd, and The Haunted Bookshop, which crams more second-hand children's and illustrated books into its minute space than anyone might believe possible.

49_ The Girton Geese

Worth taking a gander

Public art often gets a bad press, arguably because much of it is rather awful. Silly sculptures, chosen by committees and with little or nothing to do with the places they occupy, litter the land. How refreshing, then, to come across a work of art that is not only charming but also relevant to its location – and immensely practical as well.

Deciding that the village was in need of new railings to define the boundary between the car park and the churchyard, members of Girton Town Charity (GTC) took the imaginative decision to commission something that would do the job and enrich the environment as well.

They chose Cambridge-born sculptor Matthew Lane Sanderson. His particular style of direct metal sculpture uses both hand skills and modern industrial technology to create large works that manage to be robust and yet visually delicate at the same time. The design he came up with uses the theme of geese, historically associated with Girton, when flocks of domestic geese provided quills for the University. While researching for the project, Matthew also discovered that in the Middle Ages people thought that the bulbous white shells and black stalks of goose barnacles looked like the neck of a goose. When they observed these barnacles floating on pieces of driftwood they concluded that, when ripe, these shells gave birth to the geese, and the legend of a goose-bearing tree was born. So the design evolved to include a tree of life with fruits from which young geese are seen emerging.

The completed work, which is 30 metres long, is made of steel with a finish of zinc that gives a very attractive variegated patina. It is designed in sections that reflect the Fibonacci series, otherwise known as the 'Divine Proportion' used in paintings, music and architecture. So many different threads, and yet they all seem to come together in this crazy, joyous creation.

Address Cambridge Road, Girton, CB3 0PN | Getting there City Citi 6 to the top of Church Lane | Hours Unrestricted | Tip Take the opportunity to visit St Andrew's, an attractive stone church that dates from the 13th century but has had many additions over the centuries. On your way back to Cambridge, you could take in the GTC Sensory Garden on the corner of Wellbrook Way.

50__Godfrey Washington Memorial

Almost an American in Cambridge

Just inside the entrance to St Mary the Less, also known as Little St Mary's, is a memorial tablet to a Fellow of Peterhouse and vicar of the church, Godfrey Washington. His name resonates with American visitors because Godfrey was the great-uncle of George Washington, the first president of the United States. The memorial draws them to this little church because it is topped by the Washington coat of arms, which shows a black eagle sitting on a coronet, above a white shield with three red stars and two horizontal red stripes. This is thought to be the model for the Stars and Stripes, the American national flag, and the US national emblem of the eagle.

Godfrey Washington was born in York, and while one branch of his family settled in America, he remained in England. He made his career in the church and in Cambridge, where he was vicar of Cherry Hinton before becoming bursar at Peterhouse and vicar of St Mary's, where he is buried.

Little St Mary's is built on the site of an older church known as St-Peter-without-Trumpington-Gate. In 1284 the Bishop of Ely gave the church, with all its possessions and wealth, to a group of scholars lodging nearby, enabling the creation of the first Cambridge college – Peterhouse. It was rededicated to St Mary in 1352 and used as the college chapel until 1642, by which time the college had built its own chapel and St Mary's had reverted to a parish church. The building has been extensively renovated and is now a happy mix of old and new. Particularly striking are the glass entrance doors, engraved with a verse by the Metaphysical poet George Herbert.

Outside, the churchyard has been redesigned as a wild garden and nature reserve. Its winding paths, flagged and bordered with gravestones, make a very short but satisfactory walk.

Near this Place lyeth the Body of
the Late Revd Mr GODFREY
WASHINGTON of the *County*
of *York*. *Minifter* of this Church
and *Fellow* of St Peter's Colledge
Born July the 26:th 1670.
and Dyed the 28:th day of Sep.^r
1729.

Address Trumpington Street, CB2 1QG, +44 (0)1223 366202, www.lsm.org.uk | **Getting there** Any Citi bus (1–8) to town centre; Grand Arcade car park | **Hours** Open during the day. Check church noticeboard for services | **Tip** Turn down Little St Mary's Lane, which has been a residential area since 1300. The charming houses were once lodgings for the bargees who brought goods upriver. Later, the area was notorious for the prostitutes who worked from the Half Moon Inn at number 5, now long gone.

51 _ Gwen Raverat Plaque
Tribute to a charming Cambridge classic

Rather in the way Jane Austen enthusiasts see Bath through the characters and events in her novels, fans of Gwen Raverat cannot explore Cambridge without referring to her book, *Period Piece*. Subtitled *A Cambridge Childhood*, the book occupies a category of its own, somewhere between biography, social history and memoir. The people who feature in it include Cambridge luminaries and some of the best-known names of the 19th and 20th centuries. Funny, absorbing and oddly timeless, Gwen Raverat's portrayal of them in a domestic context, with all their oddities (and her own) revealed, makes them irresistible. The book has never been out of print since it was first published in 1952.

Gwen Raverat was born into a Cambridge dynasty. She was the granddaughter of Charles Darwin and the oldest child of his son George, mathematician, astronomer and a Fellow of Trinity College. He and his American wife, Maud, were key members of Cambridge's social and academic elite. Gwen grew up in the family home at Newnham Grange, now part of Darwin College, and spent much of her life in the city.

Hers was a type of late-Victorian childhood that would soon disappear. Although it was a happy one, Raverat said that at home she 'was always apt to get across the current'. She found her self-expression at the Slade School of Fine Art in London, where she perfected her skill as a wood engraver and illustrated many books for children and adults. She and her husband, the French artist Jacques Raverat, were part of the artistic and literary Bloomsbury Group, including the economist John Maynard Keynes, whose younger brother married Gwen's sister Margaret. It was a very different circle from the one she grew up in.

Unable to work following a stroke, Gwen Raverat committed suicide at the age of 71. She died in the house where she was born.

Gwen Raverat (nee Darwin)
1885 – 1957
Artist, illustrator, wood engraver and author of 'Period Piece': A Cambridge Childhood

Born and died here at Newnham Grange, the Darwin family home, now part of Darwin College

Address Darwin College, Silver Street, CB3 9EU, www.darwin.cam.ac.uk | Getting there Any Citi bus (1–8) to town centre; Grand Arcade car park, or park along Queens' Road (the Backs) (metered) | Tip Behind Darwin College is Laundress Green (where linen was once washed) and the millpond, from where the rear of Newnham Grange can be clearly seen. Here you can hire punts to take you up or down river, or just sit on the terrace at the Granta pub and watch the world go by.

52 The Heong Gallery

A stable full of culture

Bowling down the road on their bikes, or walking purposefully towards the station or the shops in the Grand Arcade, many people pass the gates of Downing College without a glance. But Downing is worth more than just a pause to admire its majestic neoclassical architecture. Unlike the popular riverside colleges, which are forced to limit access to their grounds, Downing is determined to forge closer links among the wider community. And how better to do this than with art and coffee?

Immediately inside the college entrance, fashioned from an Edwardian stable block and old bike sheds, the Heong Gallery is a mini-masterpiece of style and design. The gallery was named after Alwyn Heong, a former Downing student, who is both a collector and a passionate advocate for the visual arts. Downing engaged award-winning architects Caruso St John, who had restored the college's Grade I dining hall, to design the gallery with the same elegance and simplicity. The small, geometric space is airy and full of natural light. The broad natural oak windows, whitewashed walls and grey slate-tiled floor create a warm and intimate atmosphere. A tiny wrought-iron fireplace, recovered from the original building, provides a pleasing focal point.

The gallery aims to exhibit the best of 20th-century and contemporary art. Its first exhibition was a highly personal one, from the collection of former Tate Gallery director Sir Alan Bowness, a college alumnus. This was followed by the controversial Chinese conceptual artist Ai Weiwei's installations *Cubes* and *Trees*, and work by Richard Long, Quentin Blake and Dame Elizabeth Frink.

When you have had your fill of up-to-the-minute art, make your way to Downing's refurbished Lord Butterfield Building. The lounge-style café is a comfortable place to meet friends and you can swap books from the eclectic collection that has built up there.

Address Downing College, Regent Street, CB2 1DQ, +44 (0)1223 334800, www.dow.cam.ac.uk | Getting there Buses 1A, 3, 16A, 18, 26 or 27; Grand Arcade car park | Hours Wed–Sun noon–5pm | Tip Hobson House in St Andrew's Street is Cambridge's former Victorian police station, once also a prison and originally the 'Spinning House' (or workhouse) built by Thomas Hobson's charity. Behind the attractive frontage, work is going on to turn it into a luxury hotel.

53 Histon Road Cemetery

'Chiefly for the middle classes of society'

This quiet, attractive space is really a cemetery of two halves, grand and imposing on one side, modest on the other.

In the days before public parks were a feature of town centres, cemeteries were often seen as places where people could stroll in quiet contemplation, but they also had an educational and moral purpose. Histon Road Cemetery, formerly Cambridge General Cemetery, was opened in 1843 by Nonconformists whose chapels and churches were usually in densely populated parts of the city, with no room for burials. They did not, however, restrict the cemetery to their particular faith, and it was one of the first in the country to welcome those of any religion or none. J. C. Loudon, a leading Victorian garden designer, drew up the plans, although he did not live to see them implemented. Architect Edward Buckton Lamb designed the lodge and the chapel – only the lodge remains, but the outline of the chapel can still be seen in the grass at the centre of the cemetery.

There are stark reminders of a past era here. Out of 8,245 interments, 1,500 were stillborn babies and infants, and a further 952 children died before their 12th birthday. More cheerfully, there are 7 centenarians. In the end, the cemetery came to serve the whole community, not just the middle classes, but the difference in the memorials to the great and good of the city stand out – worthies such as Mitcham and Thoday, whose names will be familiar to many Cambridge residents because of the streets named after them.

The original evergreen trees have recently been joined by a range of other attractive specimens. Wild flowers and wildlife (including the local black squirrel) abound. A dedicated team of local residents works tirelessly to ensure that this tranquil spot is maintained, while keeping its integrity. Strolling around the cemetery, it's easy to forget the deafening traffic of Victoria Road and Histon Road, just a hedge away.

Address Histon Road, CB4 3QE, www.histonroadcemetery.org | **Getting there** Citi 8 to Histon Road corner | **Hours** Accessible 24 hours | **Tip** While looking out of his top-floor flat at 167 Victoria Road, opposite the cemetery, singer-songwriter Boo Hewerdine saw a woman on a bus who inspired the well-known song 'Patience of Angels', which became a hit for Scottish singer Eddi Reader in 1994.

54_ Hobson's Conduit

Water, plumb in the centre of town

Stepping off the pavement along Trumpington Street without looking carefully can leave you with very wet feet. Along both sides of the road are deep channels that make parking pretty hazardous, too. These carry water along Hobson's Conduit towards the city centre, and are the residual signs of an innovation that transformed the lives of Cambridge's citizens in the early 17th century.

Thomas Hobson was a wealthy entrepreneur who kept livery stables on the site where St Catharine's College now stands. His practice of lending out only the horse nearest the stable door gave rise to the expression 'Hobson's choice', meaning no choice at all. If this makes him sound unsympathetic, the impression is quite wrong – the horse nearest the door was always the longest rested, so both horse and rider benefited. Similar humanitarian principles prompted Hobson to support the construction of a conduit to bring clean drinking water into Cambridge from a number of springs to the south, improving sanitation and general health in the city.

The conduit was a rare instance of cooperation between the University and the town, which shared the cost. Four different branches fed water into the market square, college gardens and Parker's Piece, where cattle were grazed. The plan was also to clear the King's Ditch, a defensive structure that bordered the town and had become an open sewer, but here it failed. Today the conduit runs through the town, mostly underground, and is at its widest alongside the Botanic Garden. Ducks, coots and moorhens busy about here, and if you are very lucky you may spot a kingfisher. The original fountain that provided water in the market place now stands at the end of this stretch of the conduit.

Hobson set up an enduring trust to maintain the conduit, as it still does today, and his bequest ensured that his name would always be associated with the venture.

This Structure stood upon the Market Hill and served as a Conduit from 1614-1856 in which year it was Re-erected on this spot by Public Subscription

Address Hobson's Conduit runs overground along Trumpington Road (public footpath) and Trumpington Street from Long Road | Getting there Bus 26 from the city centre to the Botanic Garden; parking (metered) along Trumpington Road; otherwise the Grand Arcade car park | Hours Unrestricted | Tip St Catharine's College on Trumpington Street is named after St Catharine of Alexandria, a convert to Christianity who was condemned to death for defending her faith. She was sentenced to be broken on a wheel, but the apparatus fell to pieces when she touched it. The college features numerous catherine wheels on its buildings, gates and railings, and much satisfaction can be had in spotting them.

55 The Homecoming

Classicism versus social realism

No crushed, defeated veteran here, head bowed in thought, as is so often the case with war memorials. Cambridge's memorial to its fallen of World War I, *The Homecoming*, is a very upbeat piece of work by a most remarkable man.

Dr Robert Tait McKenzie was a Scottish-Canadian professor of physical education and physical therapy who assumed much of the medical treatment and physical training of British soldiers. He rehabilitated thousands of men suffering from physical ailments such as nerve wounds, scar tissue and joint injuries, and psychological conditions like shell shock, laying the groundwork for physiotherapy as we know it today. It was while training to be a doctor at McGill University in 1885 that he began what was to become his parallel career as a sculptor. Using athletes as models, McKenzie developed a style of sculpture reminiscent of that of classical Greece, and by 1903 his work had been accepted by the Royal Academy in London.

After the war, McKenzie largely withdrew from practising medicine and in 1920 he exhibited in London's New Bond Street, which led to the commission to sculpt the memorial for Cambridge. His model was Kenneth Hamilton, an undergraduate at Christ's College, who impressed the sculptor with his athletic physique. He is depicted as a soldier in the Cambridgeshire Regiment uniform of a private, a rifle slung over his shoulder. This fine young man strides purposefully townwards, his head turned towards the station as if looking for his comrades. In one hand he holds his helmet and a rose, in the other the butt of his rifle. On his knapsack are a captured German helmet and a laurel wreath – symbols of victory. On the plinth below is the University motto, which translates as 'From this place we gain enlightenment and precious knowledge'. From the bench beside the monument you can sit and contemplate what knowledge we have gained.

Address Junction of Station Road and Hills Road (CB1) | Getting there Citi 1, 3 or 7; Busway A and C | Tip Carry on south on Hills Road, over the railway bridge, for a view of one of the most vilified new buildings in Cambridge – the Marque – shortlisted in 2014 for the annual Carbuncle Cup, an architectural award for the worst building in the UK.

56 IWM Duxford

A museum in the air

Duxford means planes and to many it will always be associated with the World War II flying ace Douglas Bader, who led the controversial Big Wing fighter interception force from the airfield during the Battle for France in the summer of 1940, and the Battle of Britain later that year.

The aerodrome at Duxford was built during World War I and became an RAF base in 1924. It was home to the famous No. 19 Squadron, one of the first to take delivery of the new Spitfire in 1938. The squadron operated from Duxford until 1943, boosted by pilots from Australia, Canada, New Zealand, Czechoslovakia and Poland, when the airfield was handed over to the US Air Force for the remainder of the war.

Its inland position meant RAF Duxford was less useful in peacetime, and its future was uncertain until 1976, when the Imperial War Museum (IWM) bought the site to store, repair and display planes and tanks that were too large for London. IWM Duxford quickly became a centre for aviation history. Beyond its own historic interest, the site contains an outstanding range of exhibits, and its air shows, in which vintage and state-of-the-art planes take part, are held throughout the year, drawing thousands of spectators.

Duxford has been a film location in the past, and with planes taking off and landing all around, as well as the sounds and smells of the static exhibits, you might feel you really are on a film set. To get the most out of the museum you need to make a day of it, as there is so much to see. An annual pass is available for enthusiasts who want to make several visits. Otherwise, there are excellent online audio and visual resources to supplement the museum's exhibits on its website.

Be prepared for a lot of walking (the facilities for people with disabilities are excellent), bring a picnic, or take a break at one of the cafés and restaurants on site.

Address Duxford, CB22 4QR, +44 (0)207 416 5000, www.iwm.org.uk | Getting there
By car via the A 505 or M 11; Citi 7 from city centre or the train station at Whittlesford.
Special buses to the airfield on show days | Hours Daily 10am – 6pm | Tip If it's planes in
the air you want, one of the best times to visit Duxford is the day before an air show when
the pilots are rehearsing, and you can see virtually the whole show for the usual museum
entrance fee.

57 Institute of Astronomy

A date with the solar system

The Institute of Astronomy was formed in 1972 from three eminent institutions: the Institute of Theoretical Astronomy, the Solar Physics Observatory and the Cambridge University Observatory. The last one of these, and the oldest, was established in 1823 on the current site and is still housed in an elegant building in the revived Greek style. The new building was founded in 1966 by its director, the controversial cosmologist Sir Fred Hoyle, who coined the term 'Big Bang' to describe how the universe began.

On crisp winter Wednesday nights, couples and families with young children can be spotted emerging from the darkness of a car park and surging towards the Institute of Astronomy buildings to experience for themselves the wonders of the night sky. The keenest among them arrive early to hear a short talk by one of the Institute's staff members on some aspect of astronomy, such as 'Planet-eating white dwarfs', 'Astrophysics for Supervillains' or 'How clumpy is the dark matter in the Milky Way?' Later, they will be joined by many more people who just want some expert input to help them identify the stars and planets.

A queue forms outside the domed building as people wait patiently to look through the Northumberland Telescope. Donated in 1833 by the Duke of Northumberland, it was for many years one of the world's largest refracting telescopes, and although no longer used by researchers at the Institute, it continues to have a useful life on Public Observing Nights.

The smaller Thorrowgood Telescope, which is also popular with Wednesday night stargazers, dates back to 1864 and has been on extended loan to the Institute since 1929. Other smaller and more modern telescopes are erected outside, and screens transmit images while roving astronomers with clip-on mics point out constellations and answer the public's questions.

Address Madingley Rise, Madingley Road, CB3 0HA, +44 (0)1223 337548, www.ast.cam.ac.uk | **Getting there** Citi 4 (although infrequent in the evenings) to opposite J. J. Thomson Avenue | **Hours** Oct–Mar, Wed 7–9pm. Talks go ahead whatever the weather, but observing will only take place if the sky is clear (check website); group visits can also be arranged | **Tip** If you are visiting by car or bicycle, the attractive village of Coton is only a short distance away, and The Plough will make a good stopping-off place for a reviving drink.

58 Jesus Green Lido
Making a splash

No matter what the weather or the water temperature are like, there is a loyal band of hardy swimmers keen to eat up the lengths. The Lido used to close for the winter, but it's now open year round (wet suits advisable when the temperature goes below 14).

The heyday of the lido was the 1920s and 1930s, when 169 were built across the country to cater for the popularity of swimming outdoors. In Cambridge, until that time, swimming in the Cam near Sheep's Green and Coe Fen was the only option, unless you were fortunate enough to be a member of a college with its own pool. Many lidos have been demolished, having fallen victim to the preference for warmer indoor pools, the rise of cheap foreign holidays and the relentless march of developers, but those that remain are enjoying a renaissance.

Jesus Green Lido was built in 1923 on Jesus Green to be near local schools and so accessible to children, discouraging them from swimming in the river, which was judged dangerous. It made use of the natural flow of water above Jesus Lock to keep the baths pure and clean. Constructed parallel to the Cam, it was designed to mimic the experience of river swimming, and is significantly longer than it is wide: at 100 yards in length (but just 33 yards wide), it is the longest outdoor pool in the country. Although it has been upgraded in recent years, with new changing rooms, an ice cream kiosk and a sauna, all the features of the original design are still in evidence. There is a sloping paved area for sun worshippers at one end, and at the other a shaded grassy area, popular with families. On one side there are wooden seats and on the other is a grass bank, shaded by trees.

Whether you want to plunge energetically into the pool and swim lengths or simply splash around and then relax with a book, the Lido will leave you feeling thoroughly energised.

Address Chesterton Road, CB4 3AX, +44 (0)1223 302579, www.jesusgreenlido.org |
Getting there Bus 95 or Citi 4 to opposite Carlyle Road | Hours May–Sept, daily; hours
vary throughout the season. Check website for details | Tip To relax and warm up after your
swim, The Boathouse, just across from the Lido on Chesterton Road, is a comfortable and
attractive pub. Its large tiered terrace looks out over the river and Jesus Green.

59 Kettle's Yard

'A way of life'

The creation and establishment of Kettle's Yard must surely be one of the most unusual events in museum history in Britain. It was all down to Jim Ede.

A schoolboy at The Leys School in Cambridge, Jim went on to study painting at Newlyn Art School and, after World War I, he attended the Slade in London. His life changed dramatically when he was offered the position of assistant curator at the Tate Gallery. During his time as curator in the 1920s and '30s, he got to know many of the country's leading artists, and formed a strong friendship with the painters Ben and Winifred Nicholson.

What is now known as Kettle's Yard was the home of Jim and Helen Ede between 1958 and 1973. They had acquired it as a set of derelict cottages and restored it with a view to creating 'a haven of rest in an over-complicated life'. By the time the Edes retired to Edinburgh, the house had become the extraordinary statement about contemporary art that we see today. The Edes left the house, with all its pictures, ornaments and sculpture, exactly as they had lived in it, complete with all its furniture, furnishings and a wonderful collection of books. Such was the feeling of being in a real house, rather than a museum, that a visitor once reported finding a letter to Jim Ede from T. E. Lawrence, tucked into a book about Lawrence of Arabia.

In 1966 Jim Ede gifted the house and all its contents to the University for the benefit of undergraduates and to stimulate interest in contemporary art. In 1970 the house was extended and a gallery added for modern and contemporary exhibitions. In addition to the visual arts, Kettle's Yard is also well known in the city for its programme of musical events and recitals. The house and gallery reopened in 2018 following extensive renovation that resulted in the creation of an education wing, improved exhibition galleries, a new entrance and a café.

Address Castle Street, CB3 0AQ, +44 (0)1223 748100, www.kettlesyard.co.uk | Getting there Bus 1A, 2, 5, 6 or 55 from Drummer Street; Grand Arcade car park | Hours Gallery Tue–Sun 11am–5pm; House Tue–Sun noon–5pm (timed tickets for the house available from the information desk, but pre-booking is recommended) | Tip Walk back down the hill towards Magdalene Bridge and visit the atmospheric Pickerel Inn, which dates back to 1540 and in its time has been a brothel and an opium den. In the 19th century, there were 31 inns and beer houses between Bridge Street and Magdalene Street; today, only the Pickerel remains.

60__The Lawrence Room

Mummy dearest

The English suffragist and educational reformer Emily Davies set up England's first residential college for women in 1869, in Hitchin. Three years later, enough money had been collected through fundraising for the purchase of a spacious site on the outskirts of Girton village, to the north of Cambridge – a site considered to be 'near enough for male lecturers to visit but far enough away to discourage male students from doing the same'. The college is a showpiece by Alfred Waterhouse in the Victorian Gothic Revival style – all red brickwork, towers and turrets, with attractive terracotta details.

The small, attractive Lawrence Room museum, situated inside the main college building, was established in 1934 in memory of Amy Lawrence, a Girton natural scientist, by her sisters. The core of the museum consists of some well-preserved Anglo-Saxon exhibits, unearthed when workmen were preparing the grounds for a new tennis court. Other exhibits have been donated, and include some splendid Tanagra figurines, Mycenean antiquities, paintings (by Stanley Spencer, Winifred Nicholson and Edward Ardizzone, among others), a diptych by the 14th-century Sienese artist Francesco di Vannuccio, and furniture and artefacts from across the world.

The star of the museum's show, and so very appropriate given Girton's antecedents, is a beautifully preserved Roman portrait mummy labelled Hermione. Dating from the first century A.D., the mummy was discovered a little over 100 years ago in Egypt by the archaeologist William Flinders Petrie. Hermione is remarkable for the beauty of her portrait and for the inscription on her face, which translates as 'Hermione, teacher'. The archaeologist was keen for this special mummy to go to a women's college and so, after a brief and highly successful fundraising effort, Hermione arrived at Girton in 1911. More fundraising acquired a new case for her, and she holds pride of place in the museum's collection today.

Address Girton College, Huntingdon Road, CB3 0JG, +44 (0)1223 338999 (College) or 766672 (Lawrence Room), www.girton.cam.ac.uk | Getting there Citi 5 or 6 to opposite Girton Road | Hours Thu 2–4pm; other times by appointment (24 hours' notice required) | Tip In Girton High Street, the old red telephone box (a post-1956 'Pepys Kiosk') has been given a complete makeover and now operates as a book swap point. Bring along a book to donate and take one away with you.

61__The Leper Chapel

Are you going to Stourbridge Fair?

Although leprosy is not an especially contagious disease, throughout history the social stigma was such that lepers were widely feared and quarantined in leper colonies. Often these were far from habitation – on a mountain or a main road on the outskirts of a town where the lepers could beg for alms.

Stourbridge Hospital was set up some time between 1125 and 1150 on a prominent site so that 'passers-by may witness the exhibition of divine justice and admire the piety of the hospital's benefactors'. So it wasn't enough just to give money – the burgesses wanted to be seen to be doing it. By the mid-12th century a chapel, the Chapel of St Mary Magdalene, had been built for the hospital and was possibly used for the sick and dying lepers to sleep in.

Royal patronage began with King Henry II, and in 1211 King John gave the hospital a charter granting the lepers permission to hold a three-day fair on their land each September. This came to be known as Stourbridge Fair, and the income derived from it became a vital source of funds for the leper community. The fair grew to be one of the largest in Europe and later extended over more than three weeks, spreading down to the river where barges offloaded their wares from Kings Lynn. Goods were displayed by type, giving rise to names that live on in the area today: Garlic Row, Mercers Row and Oyster Row. Horseshoes and oyster shells are still finding their way to the surface even today.

The fair's decline began in the 18th century and the last fair was held in 1933, but each September you can step back into medieval times, as alchemists, pedlars, minstrels and dancers provide entertainment at the re-enactment of the fair, in front of the Leper Chapel. It now provides an atmospheric setting for community art exhibitions, theatre and concerts, but truly comes into its own during candlelit retellings of ghost stories.

Address Barnwell Junction, Newmarket Road, CB5 8JJ, +44 (0)1223 243830, www.cambridgeppf.org | **Getting there** Citi 3 to Coldhams Common, Ditton Walk or Newmarket Road Park & Ride | **Hours** Normally viewable from the outside only, although there are regular open days; check website for these, and for events in the chapel | **Tip** On Newmarket Road, in a little square outside the Tesco store, is the attractive Cambridge Gas Company War Memorial, with its octagonal shrine and domed roof, erected in 1921 and moved to its current position when the gas works were demolished in 2000. It is 'In remembrance of our fellow workers who fell in the Great War 1914–1918', and was later inscribed with the names of the fallen of World War II.

62 Lloyds Bank

A magnificent temple to money

Until the land around Cambridge Station began to be developed a few years ago, and new tall blocks started to go up, the crenellated tower of Foster's Mill (also known as Spiller's Mill) dominated the skyline. It was erected there by the wealthy Foster family, who had been prevented by the University from constructing their own railway lines to any of their three mills. So they built their mill right by the station instead.

In 1804, brothers Ebenezer and Robert Foster, both at one time mayors of Cambridge, founded a bank for their mill workers in Bridge Street that later moved to Trinity Street. By the end of the 19th century the company had outgrown its premises, and commissioned a new and magnificent building from architect Alfred Waterhouse, who also designed Girton College, but is perhaps most famous for London's Natural History Museum. The building that stands on the corner of Sidney Street, now Lloyds, still bears the Foster name above the main entrance. Built in the Dutch Renaissance style, it uses extravagant stripes of ashlar and red brick to great effect. The round arch doorway is topped by a niche in which a thoughtful looking naked *putto* (with a strategically placed shield) appears to stand guard, and above all of this is an elaborate hexagonal clock tower with a tiled spire.

As if that wasn't impressive enough, the interior is simply breathtaking in its grandeur: the domed octagonal banking hall is entered from the street through archways clad in gleaming faïence tiles. The walls also feature moulded faïence tiles in a variety of relief patterns, all in muted shades of cream, beige and mossy green. These were produced by Burmantofts of Leeds, whose very distinctive style set it apart from other potteries of its era.

But don't be tempted to photograph inside – bank staff will politely tell you that for security reasons, this is not allowed.

Address 1–3 Sidney Street, CB2 3HQ | Getting there Citi 1, 2, 3, 5, 6 or 8 to Hobson Street; Grand Arcade car park | Hours Tue–Fri 9am–5pm, Sat 9am–3pm | Tip On the other side of the road, opposite Next, is an unusual wooden war memorial situated in the grounds of Holy Trinity Church. It commemorates the 45 members of the church who gave their lives in World War I, and invites passers-by to 'enter in for rest and shelter' (although ironically it seems to be padlocked most of the time these days).

63__The Market

Books, bikes, beetroot and bread

While it might have become overshadowed by the University, Cambridge was a busy market town long before any scholars and students arrived. Old street names give an idea of the goods sold in the different parts of the market – fish on Peas Hill (nothing to do with peas, but a corruption of *pisces*, the Latin for fish), baked goods in Petty Cury ('Little Cookery') and meat in Short Butcher Row (now Wheeler Street).

Before 1849 the market stretched right from Petty Cury to Peas Hill in an L-shape. But all that was changed by the Great Fire of Cambridge that destroyed several houses on Market Hill (which is not a hill at all) and seriously damaged many more. The whole area was cleared, and by 1855 had become a large open rectangle with an ornate fountain at its centre.

During the week, the market consists of around 100 stalls selling just about everything you could want, including plants, flowers, tea and coffee, artisan breads, cheese, fruit and veg, meat, fish, T-shirts, hats, books, vinyl records, sweets, jewellery, souvenirs and health foods of all kinds. Post Covid-19 lockdown, and the market isn't quite what is was. Early in the week, there can be empty stalls, but towards the weekend it fills out and bustles with life, although it does seem that what most people are after is a recent addition – street food stalls.

On Sundays and bank holiday Mondays, the stallholders of the Arts, Crafts and Local Produce Market take over, and the pace of the market slows down. Everyone who trades here makes or creates their own products. The organic vegetable stall has people queuing round the block from early on, and business is brisk at the other food stalls. Local farmers sell organic meat (including beef from the Red Poll cattle that graze on Midsummer Common), cakes and cheeses, while talented local craftsmen and women display their paintings, pottery, sculpture and photographs.

Address Market Square, CB2 3QJ | Getting there Bus 199 to opposite Bene't Street; Grand Arcade car park | Hours Mon – Sat 10am – 4pm; Arts and Crafts Market Sun 10am – 4pm | Tip Behind the Guildhall is the Old Library, built in 1884, now home to The Giggling Squid. The interior of this Italianate building has largely been preserved, but with the addition of striking Thai floral decor. Diners can admire the tall marble columns supporting a domed roof that seems to float above clerestory windows.

64 Michaelhouse Centre

Delicious things in medieval Cambridge

If you are looking for a place to rest between college visits or during a shopping trip – or just to open your laptop and make a coffee and brownie last for an hour or so – head for the café at the Michaelhouse Centre.

Although St Michael's church looms over Trinity Street, the café entrance, through a gate in the railings, is easy to miss. But the understated exterior is misleading, because inside it the café occupies a large, light, open space, on two levels. The home-made food is simple and seasonal, with all ingredients supplied by local or East Anglian companies. Far more than a café, if not quite a restaurant, Michaelhouse is popular with customers of all ages and a great place for people-watching.

The centre takes its name from the original Michaelhouse, which was the second college to be founded in Cambridge, in 1323, and whose land extended from Trinity Street down to the river. Michaelhouse thrived for over two centuries until it was threatened by Henry VIII's ruthless seizure of the land and wealth of religious foundations. Many colleges in Oxford and Cambridge were in danger at this time. But in 1546 Henry decreed that Michaelhouse and a number of smaller hostels could keep their money and property if they merged to form a larger college in his honour. Nominally founded by the king, Trinity College actually cost him nothing.

There has been a St Michael's on the old college site in Trinity Street since the 13th century. In 2002, the Michaelhouse Centre was opened as a community exhibition and performance space and café. Occasional religious services are still held in the building, and the chapel where Hervey de Stanton, the founder of the original Michaelhouse, is buried is a space for meditation and prayer. Many visitors are drawn to Michaelhouse because it is the setting for Susanna Gregory's bestselling *Matthew Bartholomew Chronicles*.

Address St Michael's Church, Trinity Street, CB2 1SU, +44 (0)1223 693216, www.michaelhousecafe.co.uk | Getting there Bus 199 to opposite Bene't Street; Grand Arcade car park | Hours Mon–Sat 9am–5pm, Sun noon–4pm | Tip Trinity Street is the original High Street of Cambridge, and its shops represent a wide range of trades. There has been a bookshop at 1 Trinity Street continuously since 1581 (since 1992 the Cambridge University Press bookshop), making it the oldest bookshop site in Britain.

65 Midsummer Common

Fireworks, fairs and an armadillo

Midsummer Common is an area of ancient common land close to the city centre, more or less contiguous with Jesus Green and Stourbridge Common. It was grazing land for hundreds of years and was also, as its name implies, the site of a midsummer fair from the early 13th century. Originally a trade fair, the midsummer fair was a general debauch, much to the University's disapproval, and over time morphed into a horse-trading and pottery-trading site before becoming a funfair, as it is today. The annual Strawberry Fair (see ch. 103) is also held here, and the fireworks for Guy Fawkes' Day. Houseboats moor along its south bank and the town and University boathouses line the opposite bank.

The common is a busy place, crisscrossed with paths to different parts of the city, and it often shows signs of wear and tear. The council has invested significantly in its upkeep and trees have been planted to return it to its traditional appearance. The practice of grazing cattle on the common was revived in 2007 with the aim to improve the quality of the land, and now for several months of the year a small herd of bullocks roams freely here. A recent survey confirmed 14 types of tree on the common and 76 species of wild flower – encouraging signs.

A sign of a different kind is the splendid, copper-roofed public lavatory to the west of the common. Nicknamed 'The Armadillo' because of its shape, this energy-saving eco-loo captures rainwater and has sensor-controlled lighting. It also houses a Pinder Room – storage space for the straw and equipment the official pinder, who looks after the grazing cattle, needs to inspect, look after and move the steers.

The bucolic atmosphere of Midsummer Common today reveals nothing of less happy periods of Cambridge's history. During the Black Death in the 14th century and the Great Plague 200 years later, plague pits were dug here, for the victims' bodies.

Address CB5 8DJ, www.cambridge.gov.uk/midsummer-common | **Getting there** Any Citi bus to town centre; Grafton Centre car park | **Tip** Fair Street, off Maid's Causeway, was the route townspeople took to the Midsummer Fair. On the side of the house on the corner you can see the parish boundary marks ('HTP' for Holy Trinity Parish) and the dates when members of the community 'beat the parish bounds', checking all was well.

66 Milestones to Barkway

The tale of a mouse and a hare

As well as having been at the heart of Cambridge for over 800 years, Great St Mary's Church is the official centre of Cambridge, with a plaque just below the west tower that marks the spot. From this point, there is a series of 16 milestones that stretch along the old Roman road all the way to Barkway in Essex – the first to be erected since Roman times.

The first stone can be found where the old London road crosses Vicar's Brook by a brick culvert south of Brooklands Avenue known as Stonebridge, which is possibly a contraction of Milestone Bridge. On the stone are the words 'I Mile to Great Saint Maries Church, Cambridge A.D. MDCCXXVIII', together with the crescent arms of Trinity Hall. The stones were initiated by the will of Dr William Mowse, a Master of Trinity Hall during the mid-16th century, who left £1,000 for charitable purposes. His executor, Robert Hare, was responsible for deciding how to invest the surplus from the estate and, adding £600 himself, bought the manor of Wallpool, the rental from which was to be used for the maintenance of the roads around Cambridge. Dr William Warren, a later trustee and a Fellow of Trinity Hall, had the series of milestones installed in 1728.

In 1940 the government decreed that all place names should be removed to impede the enemy in the event of invasion. All the stones were laid face down and hidden in the grass verge, although most of them were re-erected after the war and are still there today.

Trinity Hall revived the tradition, and enjoyed a small private in-joke, when it commissioned a milestone for the opening of its new Wychfield buildings in 2006. Cut in Portland stone by the Cardozo Kindersley workshop, the stone shows that it is 2006 metres from Trinity Hall and 50 metres from the Wychfield entrance. The red painted nails on the pointing hands might have startled Dr Mowse, had he been around to see them.

I
MILE TO
GREAT SAINT
MARIES CHURCH
CAMBRIDGE

Address (66a) Trumpington Road, where it meets Chaucer Road; (66b) Trinity Hall Wychfield Site, 1 Storey's Way, CB3 0DZ, +44 (0)1223 339029, www.trinhall.cam.ac.uk | Getting there First milestone is situated on Trumpington Road: Bus 26 to opposite Brooklands Avenue; Wychfield Site: Citi 5 or 6 to near Richmond Road | Hours Accessible 24 hours | Tip The gardens of Trinity Hall's Wychfield Site on Storey's Way are a delight: winding gravel pathways, exuberant spring flowers on Cherry Tree Mound, a sunken garden and a woodland walk with plenty of interesting wildlife.

2006m

50m

AD MMVI

67__ The Mill

Of pints and punts

Visitors to the UK quickly realise, if they did not know already, that much of British social life revolves around public houses. As an ancient city, Cambridge has been and still is home to a huge variety of traditional ale houses, but The Mill must rate as one of the most interesting and characterful pubs in the city.

It looks out over two rivers – the lower river known as the Cam passes through the Backs, while the upper river is the Granta, which flows down from Grantchester. Although it has no outside seating of its own, there are two broad walls opposite that are perfect for sitting on; watching the gentle stream of human traffic along the river is an occupation in itself. Just beyond is Laundress Green, so named because college washerwomen used to wash and dry laundry on the green, and summer visitors can take their food and drinks there – although they might have to share the space with some inquisitive cows.

The Mill, built in the late 18th century, has a cosy interior that looks as if it has been there for ever, although it was in fact entirely reconstructed a few years ago when, in a sorry state, it was threatened with closure. Now it is full of life, with an original 1960s' radiogram playing vinyl records in the main bar. The smaller snug houses an upright piano and a large selection of board games, and in winter there is a welcoming open fire. The impressive range of beers and cask ales is complemented by a menu of pub classics that includes good fish and chips and all manner of burgers, but there are also vegetarian, vegan and gluten-free options.

Whether you visit The Mill in winter, when you emerge feeling warm and satisfied into the Siberian wind, or in summer when the long, lazy days seem to go on for ever, and swallows skim the river as dusk falls, The Mill epitomises the very essence of what a British pub should be.

Address 14 Mill Lane, CB2 1RX, +44 (0)1223 311829, www.themillpubcambridge.com | Getting there Bus 199 to Corpus Christi, then walk down Mill Lane to the river; Grand Arcade car park | Hours Mon–Fri noon–11pm, Sat & Sun 9am–9pm | Tip Rising up behind Laundress Green is the Old Granary, once the home of Sir George Darwin, son of the eminent Charles Darwin who wrote *On the Origin of Species*. It is now part of Darwin College.

68_Mill Road
Cambridge at its alternative best

Back in the Middle Ages, Mill Road was a quiet track that led out of Cambridge through open fields to Trumpington Road. Until 1806, and the Enclosures Act, the only real landmark was the mill that gave the road its name; this stood somewhere between Covent Garden and Mawson Road, opposite Emery Street. It is believed that there was a windmill on the site as early as the 13th century, but little else is known of it until 1777, when a wooden mill was offered for sale at auction. Later rebuilt in brick, it fell into disuse after losing its sails in a storm in 1840. It was not until the early 19th century, when the colleges sold off the land they owned, that the road began to be developed.

Today, Mill Road is the cosmopolitan heart of the city, with some 20,000 residents living in the wards of Romsey, Petersfield and Coleridge. It may be a little scruffy, but the great cultural diversity of the mostly independent shops and restaurants more than makes up for any lack of smartness. Here you can almost eat your way around the world, buy ingredients from all continents, find useful household items in genuinely old-fashioned stores and just experience life in Cambridge as it is lived away from the University.

The much-anticipated Winter Fair seems to embody everything Mill Road represents. Held on the first Saturday in December, it draws in over 10,000 people from the city and surrounding area. The road is closed to traffic and is host for the day to a glorious celebration. Shops and houses throw open their doors, set up tables and try to interest passers-by in everything from falafels and cake to bric-à-brac, and information on global warming and animal welfare. Buskers and other street performers entertain the crowds, the churches hold storytelling sessions and hand out free mince pies, and the mosque welcomes families on guided tours.

If you don't know Mill Road, you don't know Cambridge.

Address From CB1 1LY (68a) to CB1 3DF (68b) | **Getting there** Bus 114 or Citi 2 | **Tip** An artwork celebrating the railway heritage of Romsey was installed at the top of Cavendish Road in 2018. The giant sculptural 'R', by Harry Gray and Will Hill, consists of a steel frame that represents railway tracks and bronze sleepers. Within the shape are departure points and destinations that have been significant in the lives of local residents.

69 Mill Road Cemetery

Some rather distinguished departed

Fans of the crime writer Alison Bruce, whose novel *The Siren* is set in and around Mill Road Cemetery, will remember her protagonist, Kimberly Guyver, describing the cemetery's shape as reminiscent of a guitar. If you could hover above the burial ground, you'd see the shape clearly – the curving paths around the perimeter forming the body, the open space in the centre the sound hole and the Norfolk Street entrance the neck.

By the early 19th century the population of Cambridge was expanding rapidly, and the burial grounds of city centre parishes had become full. Funding was provided by public subscription, and land found for a new cemetery on what was then the site of the University cricket ground (which moved to its current location at Fenner's). It was designed by Andrew Murray, who was also responsible for the layout of the new Botanic Garden. He was clearly influenced by the leading designer John Loudon, whose vision was to create 'breathing spaces' in towns for the inhabitants – places that could become public gardens once the burial grounds were full. Building was completed in 1848 and the land consecrated by the Bishop of Ely.

Around the outer pathways, deciduous trees and conifers were planted, all now large and mature. The space was divided up by straight paths that led to the mortuary chapel at the centre, one of two buildings designed by Sir George Gilbert Scott (the other is the Gothic-style flint-knapped lodge by the Mill Road entrance). The chapel was demolished in 1954, after it had fallen out of use and become unsafe, but its outline is still clearly visible in the grass.

There are many imposing monuments, alongside simpler gravestones. All around is an abundance of wildlife that makes the place a delight to wander through. In the early part of the year it is rich in flowers, and in September you can find some of the best blackberries in the city.

Address Mill Road, CB1 2AW, www.millroadcemetery.org.uk | **Getting there** Citi 2 to Mill Road, near Gwydir Street | **Hours** Accessible 24 hours | **Tip** Have a look round the back of Ditchburn Place, a little further down Mill Road, for some very imaginative, village-style social housing. The original building opened in 1838 as the Union Workhouse, later becoming a general infirmary and then a maternity hospital.

70　Museum of Archaeology and Anthropology

A museum bursting with stories

Aged 20 and suffering from bad health, Baron Anatole von Hügel set out on a curative trip to the warmer climes of the South Pacific. Following in the footsteps of his famous botanist father, he travelled first to Australia and New Zealand, and then on to Fiji, where he developed a passion for the country and its people, collecting and recording their lives as he went. While there, he made the acquaintance of two men who were later to be part of this museum's story: Sir Arthur Gordon, Fiji's first governor, and Alfred Maudslay, the explorer and collector.

Three years later in 1877 von Hügel returned to England, and then in 1883 was the surprise choice as curator of the new Museum of General and Local Archaeology. He donated his own collection to the museum, and this was enhanced with those of Gordon and Maudslay, although the existing premises were too small to display it all. This galvanised von Hügel to campaign and fundraise for a new building, and by 1913 the museum had moved to the impressive site that it inhabits today.

A major renovation in 2012 brought a striking new street entrance, behind which can be viewed a fascinating collection of objects found beneath Cambridge. Moving up to the main galleries, the Maudslay Hall is dedicated to anthropology and is built on a scale that can easily accommodate a group of huge, carved totem poles. These stand alongside a dazzling collection of historical artefacts (including objects from James Cook's voyages in the Pacific) and some modern equivalents that tell stories about our world and our relationship to it. The Andrews Gallery is devoted to archaeology and displays change frequently, but always on show are finds from major excavations and some of the earliest hominid tools ever discovered.

Address Downing Street, CB2 3DZ, +44 (0)1223 333516, www.maa.cam.ac.uk | Getting there Any Citi bus (1–8) to town centre; Grand Arcade car park | Hours Tue–Sat 10am–5pm, Sun noon–5pm | Tip If you keep your eyes glued to the ground while you're in the museum courtyard, you should spot the soles of a pair of cast-iron feet embedded in the ground. This is all that's visible of Antony Gormley's *Earthbound*: Plant, a 1,400 lb life-size sculpture of a man buried upside down.

71_Museum of Cambridge

Eel grigs and Fuzzy-Felt at the White Horse Inn

'I am inclined to think that in the University of Cambridge there is more exact knowledge of the social anthropology of, let us say, Papua, than of Pampisford.' With these words, on 3 November 1936, Sir Cyril Fox declared the new Cambridge and County Folk Museum open to the public. Three years earlier a hugely successful 'Festival of Olden Times' had been mounted in the Guildhall. Exhibits had been donated by villages in the surrounding area, and afterwards there were calls for a site to be found for a permanent collection of social history. The old White Horse Inn, which had closed earlier that year, was identified, and work began to transform it into a museum.

A delightful evocation of life as it was once lived by the people of Cambridge and the Fens, the museum is packed full of objects that will intrigue, puzzle, entertain and possibly make you think 'My granny used to have one of those'. There are more than 20,000 items, photographs and documents, all donated by the colleges and local people and displayed naturalistically by theme throughout the inn's nine rooms. In the original bar are an open fire and cooking equipment, next to the snug, where richer customers would drink – away from ordinary folk. It's now full of bizarre housekeeping devices, such as a wicker bedbug trap and fiendishly cruel mousetraps, together with an assortment of cleaning devices.

Up the perilously narrow stairs are two elegant rooms, where guests stayed (often sharing the same room, or even the same bed), full of memorabilia of some of Cambridge's notable inhabitants. Furniture and prints appear alongside false teeth, and intriguing pills and potions that claimed to cure everything from gout to ringworm, piles and scrofula. The final rooms house displays of Fenland life and childhood memorabilia – from witch bottles and thatching tools to prams and Dinky toys.

Address 2–3 Castle Street, CB3 0AQ, +44 (0)1223 355159, www.museumofcambridge.org.uk |
Getting there Bus 1, 2, 3, 8 or Citi 4 to Northampton Street; Grand Arcade car park | Hours
School holidays: Mon–Sat 10am–5pm, Sun 11am–4pm; term time: Wed–Mon | Tip Up the
hill is the 17th-century Castle Inn, popular with both students and locals. The quirky décor,
little changed over recent years, makes it a cosy place to be, and the Adnams ales are excellent.

72 Museum of Classical Archaeology

Casting about in the classical world

You could travel to Paris, queue up for hours and pay a huge entrance fee to see the Venus de Milo, or fly to Rome to see Trajan's Column, but at the Museum of Classical Archaeology, otherwise known as the Cast Gallery, you can get up close to casts of these and hundreds of other magnificent models – one of the largest collections of casts in the world. One immediate surprise is discovering that these mostly white antique figures were originally painted in bright colours, of which the museum's best-known exhibit, the Peplos Kore, is a fascinating example.

The collection was assembled so that Cambridge students of classics should have access to copies of these great works to help them with their studies. Students of art were also encouraged to draw casts as a way of seeing form and improving basic drawing skills, and many students still do so today. Originally housed in the Fitzwilliam Museum, the collection grew so large that a new home was found for it on Little St Mary's Lane, in a splendid building designed by Basil Champneys and now part of Peterhouse. Since 1983 the museum has been located within the Faculty of Classics in an airy purpose-built gallery.

The 450 exhibits of some of the best-known and important Greek and Roman sculptures are beautifully displayed as well as being sympathetically labelled, so that visitors, young or old, can understand the story behind each work. Notes around the museum and on the curator's door encourage visitors to ask questions of the staff, who are all very well informed and helpful.

The museum runs regular events for those with a particular interest in the classical world, and there is a programme of temporary exhibitions where objects are brought out of store, so with each visit there are delightful surprises.

Address First floor of the Faculty of Classics, Sidgwick Avenue, CB3 9DA, +44 (0)1223 330402, www.classics.cam.ac.uk | **Getting there** Bus 199 to Queen's Road near Malting Lane or Bus U to West Road, University Library | **Hours** Tue–Fri 10am–5pm, Sat 2–5pm (University term time only) | **Tip** Nearby in Grange Road is Selwyn College, where dogs are not allowed, so the Master's dog has been designated by the College Council as 'a Very Large Cat'. The gardens are stunning and the college buildings, designed in the Tudor Gothic style, are very much worth a visit.

73_ Museum of Technology
Green before green was ever invented

In her memoir, *Period Piece: a Cambridge Childhood*, Gwen Raverat recounts the story of a visit by Queen Victoria to Trinity College. The Queen asked the Master, Dr Whewell, 'What are all those pieces of paper floating down the river?' Not wishing to upset her majesty with the sordid truth, the quick-thinking Dr Whewell replied, 'Those, ma'am, are notices that bathing is forbidden.'

Anything and everything went straight into the river, making a terrible stench and rendering the water so impure that it was a danger to drink. In common with many parts of the country, Cambridge suffered from an outbreak of cholera – but it took people quite some time to link this to the polluted water. By 1894 pressure had built up for the creation of a system to deal with the sewage and to improve sanitation, and the Cheddars Lane Pumping Station was built. With an octagonal chimney 174 feet high, it was the tallest building for miles around, designed to send the noxious fumes high into the sky. The method used was simple but ingenious: the city's waste was brought into the pumping station by horse and cart, then tipped into burners that produced steam and pumped the waste out through underground pipes to the sewage farm at Milton, two-and-a-half miles away.

Since 1970 the building has housed the Museum of Technology, where you can take a tour around the works and see some of the fascinating and lovingly maintained machinery (as well as breathing in the evocative smell of engine oil). Their prize exhibit is the Hathorn Davey steam engine, still in working order, and when the museum is 'in steam' you will be able to experience its awesome power for yourself.

The museum reopened in 2019 after extensive redevelopment. The boiler system that runs the steam engines has been repaired, and there are now new displays together with improved visitor facilities.

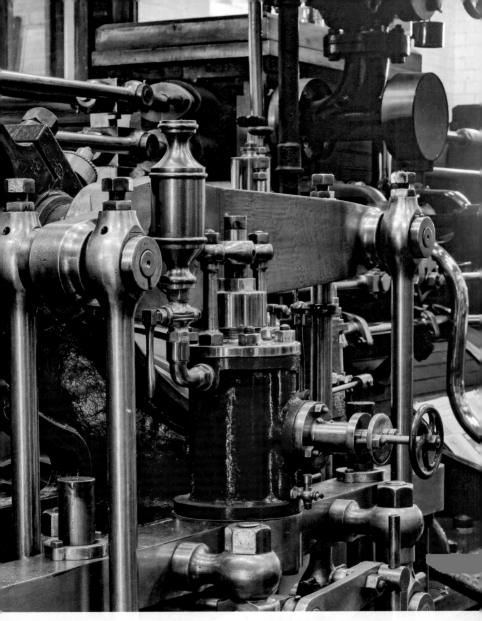

Address The Old Pumping Station, Cheddars Lane, CB5 8LD, +44 (0)1223 500652, www.museumoftechnology.com | Getting there Bus 10, 10A, 11, 12 or 196 to River Lane, then walk along the river | Hours Winter: Sat & Sun 10.30am – 4pm; summer: also open Fri | Tip On the corner where Priory Road meets Riverside is an unusual, high-aperture 'anonymous' pillar box. Through an oversight, the usual words 'Post Office' and the royal cypher were left off. Don't miss the tiny Emailerator at the base.

74 Museum of Zoology

Saving the whale (again)

The small size and relative obscurity of the departmental museums in Cambridge, many of which feature in this book, are part of their charm. Until recently, the Museum of Zoology, despite the physical bulk of some of its exhibits and an extensive refurbishment in the 1970s, could be counted among them, tucked away behind John Lewis. Now it has been transformed, thanks to a fundraising campaign and a donation of £1.8 million from the Heritage Lottery Fund.

The museum dates from 1814 when the University bought the collection of Sir Busick Harwood, Professor of Anatomy, on his death. Other major collections were added over the years, including many examples of plant and animal species, rocks and fossils that Charles Darwin collected both on his five-year voyage on HMS *Beagle* and closer to home. Over time, the collections have become a major research resource, not only for the history of life on our planet but also for the history of science itself.

The biggest draw of the museum, in all senses of the word, is the skeleton of a finback whale that beached on the south coast in 1885. It was a huge attraction *in situ* until the smell of the enormous decomposing mammal drove spectators away. The University then bought it, and for many years the skeleton hung above the entrance to the museum, which functioned as an extension of the Department of Zoology. As well as a permanent display of examples of every group of animal that has ever existed, the museum housed laboratories and was an administrative, research and teaching centre.

The revamped museum building was renamed in April 2016 in honour of the British naturalist Sir David Attenborough. The spectacular entrance is now a two-storey Whale Hall, allowing visitors to view the skeleton from all angles. New displays focus on celebrating and protecting animal diversity, and all the existing collections have been rehoused.

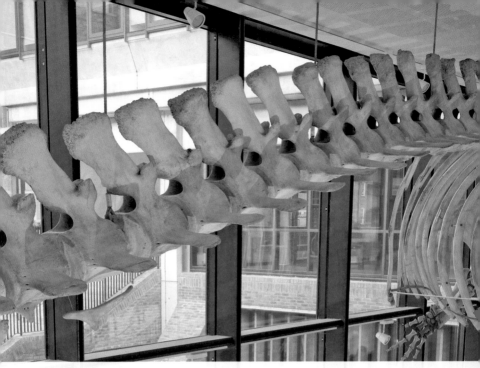

Address David Attenborough Building, Downing Place, CB2 3EJ, +44 (0)1223 336650, www.museum.zoo.cam.ac.uk | Getting there Any Citi bus (1–8) to town centre; Grand Arcade car park | Hours Tue–Sat 10am–4.30pm, Sun noon–4.30pm | Tip The Regal, on St Andrew's Street, was converted when the ABC cinema (originally the Regal cinema) closed. It is the largest pub in the UK and still looks pretty much as it always did inside. In the evenings it's a pub/club hybrid, and the prominent security staff give you a good idea of what to expect. But during the day it's an excellent place to rest and have an inexpensive and satisfying meal.

75 Mystery Mermen

A tiny church with a big puzzle

Cambridge Quayside today is a focal point for punting, eating, drinking and people-watching. But as you while away your time at one of the many cafés here, try to imagine this place as the bustling inland port and mercantile centre it was from Roman times until the mid-18th century. Coal, wine, peat and all sorts of provisions were shipped downriver from King's Lynn and unloaded on the quayside, while corn and vegetable oil were shipped back. Quayside teemed with merchants, farmers, traders, labourers and sailors – and these last might help explain the main feature of St Peter's Church, a short walk away.

This charming little church stands on rising wooded ground above Castle Street, surrounded by rather run-down modern housing. Inside is a 12th-century stone font that continues to puzzle visitors. The four-sided font is decorated with four mermen who hold out their split tails towards each other. Their plaited hair decorates the rim of the bowl. The features of only one figure remain and are clearly a renovation. The mystery is why a baptismal font is decorated with these pagan images. Could it be a repurposed mortar, originally used to grind corn? Sailors believed mermen caused storms and shipwrecks, and St Peter is the patron saint of fishermen. Does the font represent the power of the saint over these evil spirits? Did sailors and fishermen in Cambridge come here to give thanks for their safe arrival or to pray for a safe journey? Or did the association of mermen with water simply morph into a metaphor for baptism?

Whatever the explanation, the font symbolises the enduring solidity of St Peter's. The church was rebuilt sympathetically in the 18th century and many of its Saxon features were retained. Services are no longer held here, and St Peter's is now linked with St Giles', just down the road, an enormous Victorian church built in 1875 but incorporating two arches from the original 12th-century church.

Address Castle Hill, CB3 0AJ, +44 (0)1223 324442 | Getting there Bus 1A, 2, 5, 6 or 55 from Drummer Street; Grand Arcade car park | Hours Daily 10am–4pm; at other times a key is available from St Giles' Church, Castle Street, CB3 0AQ | Tip Take the slightly longer route back towards town, down Pound Hill onto Northampton Street, and stop off at The Punter, which describes itself as a 'cheerfully baggy pub'.

76 New Hall Art Collection

A discreet celebration of women's art

'Don't ask, don't get' could be the motto of the New Hall art collection at Murray Edwards College. This extraordinary accumulation of women's art, the largest in Europe, was launched in 1992 when the college President, Valerie Pearl, approached 100 British women artists to ask for donations towards a new permanent collection. Her audacity paid off, as the majority of them agreed, and now some of the best-known contemporary artists, including Paula Rego, Bridget Riley and Elizabeth Frink, are represented either through donations or later acquisitions.

Those who contributed welcomed the opportunity to participate, as women artists often felt ignored by galleries and failed to command as much exhibition space as their male counterparts. Even Maggi Hambling, who has said she doesn't approve of women's art 'in any way', doesn't take part in 'women's exhibitions', and doesn't approve of 'artists giving their work away for nothing', was persuaded to donate her painting *Gulf Women Prepare for War*, which hangs prominently in the college dining hall.

The art collection is wildly eclectic, the only unifying element the fact that all the artists are women. The collection includes representational, figurative, light-hearted and intimate works alongside highly-charged feminist, political or polemical pieces. Most of the paintings and sculptures are in public areas, and make a striking contrast to the concrete of the college's Brutalist architecture. Other parts of the college can be visited on request at the Porters' Lodge, where a full catalogue of the collection is on sale.

People come from all over the world to visit this little-publicised collection, which in size and significance is second only to the National Museum of Women in the Arts in Washington, DC. Exhibitions are held regularly throughout the year, with details available on the college website.

Address Murray Edwards College, Huntingdon Road, CB3 0DF, +44 (0)1223 762100; www.murrayedwards.cam.ac.uk | **Getting there** Citi 5 or 6 from city centre; by car, there is some parking at the college; check before arrival | **Hours** Daily 10am–6pm. You can borrow a self-guided art tour from the Porters' Lodge. Guided tours sometimes given, so telephone for details. | **Tip** The gardens at Fitzwilliam College, off Huntingdon Road, are open to the public and are a wonderful backdrop to the Brutalist architecture of the college buildings. They feature series of herbaceous beds and borders quite unlike the formal courtyard gardens of some of the older colleges. Check at the Porters' Lodge before entering.

77 _ The Old Bicycle Shop

Gearing up to deliver imaginative vegetarian food

When Howes Cycles shut up shop in 2013, after 173 years as a family business, the owners declared, 'If your surname is not Howes then you are not taking over.' But while the business left with the Howes family, the history of the premises didn't and for the new owners – the thriving City Pub Group – The Old Bicycle Shop was the obvious name for their latest venture.

The interior of this pub/restaurant retains the open space of the old bike showroom and workshop and throughout there are witty references to its previous use, from the antler trophies on the walls (made from handlebars and saddles) to the names of cocktails, including Darwin's First Ride. Howes' claimed that Charles Darwin bought a bike from the store while he was at Christ's College, but this seems unlikely as Darwin left Cambridge for the *Beagle* voyage in 1831, nearly 40 years before Howes started selling cycles. But perhaps other members of the bicycle-loving Darwin family did, as Howes was the first shop to sell cycles in the UK.

Like other City Pub Group venues (see ch. 67), The Old Bicycle Shop has its own character and serves innovative, largely vegetarian food. Meat-eaters will find delicious dishes on the menu but staff reckon that 40 per cent of their customers are vegetarian and a further 20 per cent adventurous omnivores. All beers and ciders are vegetarian (some beers are gluten-free) and some of the wines are vegan. Not forgetting the cocktails. The informal atmosphere of the pub is supported by a real commitment to sustainability. local providers are mostly used and Sustainability Sundays – when the OBS chefs devise a fixed-price, two-course menu from the previous week's surplus ingredients – are geared to minimising waste.

Keep an eye out for special events, like children's crafts during half term to keep the small people entertained, so parents can enjoy themselves too.

Address 104 Regent Street, CB2 1DP | **Getting there** Bus Citi 1, 2, 3 to Regent Street | **Hours** Daily 9.30am–11pm | **Tip** Drop in to the nearby University Arms Hotel, rebuilt and reopened in 2018, for tea or coffee, admire the view over Parker's Piece and wonder at the pristine lavatories, where Alan Bennett recites *The Wind in the Willows* on a continuous audio loop.

78_ The Orchard Tea Garden

There really is honey still for tea

Whether you stroll or cycle beside the River Cam along the path known as the Grantchester Grind, punt upstream, or arrive by car or bus, what awaits you is a rural idyll where time appears to have stood still. The Orchard's late owner, the colourful entrepreneur Robin Callan, saved it from developers and gifted it to a charitable trust to ensure that, in his words, 'God's little acre' would be preserved as part of Cambridge's cultural heritage.

The orchard in question was planted in 1868 as part of a house belonging to a Mrs Stevenson, who served tea and cake from her front room and in her garden. Some years later, a request from a group of Cambridge students to have tea served under the trees in the orchard began a trend that has since become a Cambridge tradition. The charismatic young poet Rupert Brooke lodged at Orchard House in 1909 after graduating from King's College, and it soon became the haunt of the circle of friends who became known as the Grantchester Group: the novelists Virginia Woolf and E. M. Forster, philosophers Bertrand Russell and Ludwig Wittgenstein, the economist John Maynard Keynes and the artist Augustus John.

The tiny museum that told the story of Brooke's life displayed many artefacts alongside a few of his belongings, books, poems, photographs and letters closed some years ago, but these objects can still be seen in the restaurant. Among these are his pocket diary and the binoculars he took with him when he was sent to fight at Gallipoli (tragically he died of sepsis on board ship before ever being deployed). Also on view are many photographs of the luminaries with whom Brooke associated.

Relax in a deckchair under the fruit trees, enjoy a cup of tea or a light lunch, listen to the bees and the pigeons, experience a slower pace of life and contemplate this lovely spot that remains 'forever England'.

Address The Orchard, Tea Garden, 47 Mill Way, CB3 9ND, +44 (0)1223 840230, www.theorchardteagarden.co.uk | **Getting there** Bus 18 or 18A from Drummer Street or Lensfield Road, but the journey on foot or by bike or car would be infinitely easier | **Hours** Daily from 10am; summer and winter closing times vary; closed 24 and 25 December | **Tip** The beautiful St Andrew and St Mary's Church in Grantchester is renowned for its connection with the poet Rupert Brooke, and its clock hands standing at ten to three. On Boxing Day, Grantchester is packed with crowds who come to see the barrel race, when villagers enthusiastically race huge barrels down the high street.

79__Our Lady and the English Martyrs

'The Catholic'

Since 1890 Our Lady and the English Martyrs has dominated the junction of Hills Road and Lensfield Road. Better known to most Cambridge residents as a location ('Meet you by the Catholic') than as a place to worship, it is one of the largest and arguably the finest Roman Catholic churches in the United Kingdom, with a history as fascinating as its architecture.

The architects Dunn and Hansom of Newcastle were engaged by Mrs Yolande Marie Louise Lyne-Stephens, the widow of a wealthy industrialist. Her husband Stephens Lyne-Stephens was a banker and Member of Parliament, reputed to be the richest commoner in England, his fortune having been inherited through the family's Portuguese glass factory and a patent for movable dolls' eyes.

Yolande, whose birth name was Pauline Duvernay, was born outside Paris in 1813, and became a star of the ballet at the Paris Opéra. On moving to London she performed in the 1830s at Drury Lane, where audiences were captivated by her delicacy, elegant technique and great beauty. Lyne-Stephens fell in love with her, and in 1837, at the height of her career, she retired to marry him. Sadly, they had no children, and Stephens' death 23 years later left Yolande a very wealthy but lonely woman. The remainder of her life was devoted to spending her vast fortune on philanthropy, building many monuments, of which her most lavish gift was Cambridge's Catholic church – a controversial presence in 19th-century Cambridge.

Built in the Gothic Revival style to a traditional cruciform structure, the church has superb stained glass and a tall, spacious interior, best viewed from the gateway in the iron screen that divides the nave from the ante-chapel. St Alban and St Thomas Becket can be seen on either side of the north entrance.

Address Hills Road, CB2 1JR | **Getting there** Bus 18, 26 or 75 to the junction of Hills Road and Lensfield Road | **Hours** Mon – Fri 7am – 6.15pm, Sat 8am – 7pm, Sun 7am – 8pm | **Tip** On the corner of Hills Road and Coronation Street is Maison Clément, a real French pâtisserie selling the most delicious tarts and pastries.

80___Paradise

A little piece of heaven on earth

There can be few urban environments in the world where cattle graze along the riverside, on open land, as they do in the heart of Cambridge.

At the bottom of Fen Causeway as you cross the road, having dodged the cattle and negotiated rickety wooden bridges across the marsh of Coe Fen, you can continue to follow the river in the direction of Grantchester. A short distance further on, still well within the central city, you pass a very substantial riverside play area, full of children at all times of the year. But then you will come upon a magical natural woodland and wetland habitat that has survived unchanged for centuries, known as Paradise.

Paradise is a small island created by several minor tributaries of the River Cam that define its wetland nature. The area often floods, but boardwalks have recently been installed to make the area more accessible. Here you will find several species of mature willow trees, always associated with water, and a rich and varied assortment of nesting birds, plants and insects. If you are visiting Paradise in midsummer you may well be able to join a bat walk, where experts will point out two types of pipistrelle, Daubenton's bat, and others if you are lucky.

As well as watching punts glide lazily along the river towards Grantchester, you will almost certainly spot enthusiastic and hardy swimmers in the river at just about any time of year in Paradise. But this is not without its dangers: it was here in 1811 that Byron's libertine friend Charles Matthews became entangled in weeds and drowned. After little more than 500 yards the pathway through this area of exquisite natural beauty will bring you to a group of houses at the bottom of Owlstone Road. However, in another short walk to the bottom of Eltisley Avenue you will be reunited with the footpath that will take you to Grantchester through the more open water meadows.

Address By Lammas Land car park, Newnham, CB2 | **Getting there** Bus 18 or 75 to Newnham (Grantchester Street), but more enjoyably reached on foot or bike | **Tip** The Lammas Land recreation ground has probably the best play equipment in Cambridge, for both young and older children. There is also a large shallow paddling pool and free table tennis (bring your own bats and balls).

81　Pembroke College Chapel

Where Wren first spread his wings

Stand outside Pembroke College and enjoy your first view of the elegant chapel, the first classical college chapel to be built in Cambridge. Its west façade can be seen from the street, beside a much later addition to the college, by Alfred Waterhouse, about whose contributions to Pembroke the architectural historian Sir Nikolaus Pevsner had little good to say: '[I]n every case where he added at Pembroke he spoiled something that was already there.'

Pembroke College was founded in 1347 by Mary de St Pol, who by romantic (and dubious) tradition became a widow on her wedding day when her husband was killed jousting. It comprised a chapel, kitchen, dining hall, Master's lodge and student rooms, all forming today's Old Court. The original chapel, which needed permission to be built from the pope, is still there and is now known as the Old Library.

The rise to power of the English clergyman and scholar Matthew Wren was meteoric in Charles I's reign, but his later toughness on Puritans led to his imprisonment in the Tower of London. He vowed, should he be released, to pay for a new chapel for Pembroke, his old college. This he did, and chose his nephew Christopher Wren to accomplish the task for him. At the time, Christopher was professor of astronomy at Oxford, but had an interest in architecture that had grown out of his study of engineering and physics, so the fact that building the chapel was his first job makes it all the more remarkable. The precise wooden model he made is still in the possession of the college.

Consecrated in 1665, the chapel is airy and full of light, from great windows that allow the superb plaster ceiling to be viewed in its full magnificence. Colour is concentrated in the fine altar painting, a copy of Federico Barocci's *Entombment*, and in the stained glass added in 1906 in memory of the mathematician George Stokes.

Address Trumpington Street, CB2 1RF, +44 (0)1223 338100, www.pem.cam.ac.uk |
Getting there Any Citi bus (1–8) to town centre; Grand Arcade car park | Hours Daily,
as for college opening hours, but college closed during exam periods, so check at Porters'
Lodge | Tip Look out for the Wednesday lunchtime concerts at the Downing Place United
Reformed Church (www.downingplaceurc.org), as well as their series of events and classes
that range from knitting and Kung Fu to lunch club.

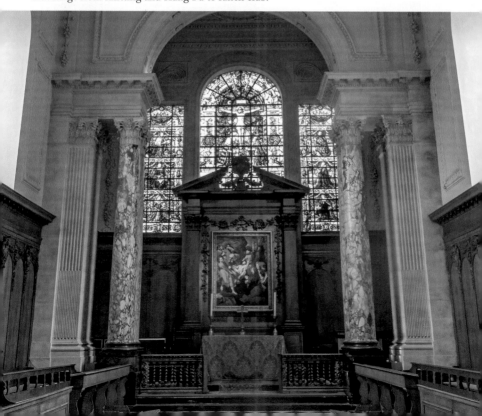

82 The Pepys Library

'For the benefit of posterity'

The great 17th-century naval administrator Samuel Pepys is perhaps best known for the diary he kept that chronicled momentous events of the Restoration period, blended with fascinating details of what life was really like for a gentleman of the time. The diary was written in a form of shorthand called tachygraphy, and was only deciphered more than a hundred years after Pepys' death.

Even if the diary had never been written, Pepys would still be remembered as an exceedingly able civil servant, a friend of many intellectuals of his time, and the creator of a superb library. Pepys assembled these books throughout his life, but on his retirement from the Navy was able to devote more time to his collection. His principle in collecting these works together was that 'a private library should comprehend in fewest books and least room the greatest diversity of subjects, styles and languages its owner's reading will bear'. He bequeathed it to Magdalene, his old college, on his death, provided that they accept his conditions.

Housed in an attractive long, narrow room with paintings on every wall, the collection of 3,000 books is displayed in 12 handsome glass-fronted cases (called 'presses') and in Pepys' own Library Table. The neat arrangement of the books and their immaculate leather bindings is very striking, but Pepys was nothing if not a perfectionist. Books are arranged by height, rather than by subject matter, and Pepys pioneered a system of cataloguing that enables any book to be found quickly and easily.

For the book enthusiast, the display cases contain some fascinating examples: Newton's *Principia*, a translation of Ovid's *Metamorphoses* made by William Caxton in 1480 from a French version, and two of the Anthony Rolls – illuminated manuscripts that provided a visual record of ships of the English Tudor navy – given to Pepys by King Charles II.

Address Magdalene College, Magdalene Street, CB3 0AG, +44 (0)1223 332115, www.magd.cam.ac.uk | **Getting there** Bus 1A, City 3 or 6; Grand Arcade car park | **Hours** Tours on selected Friday mornings (bookable in advance); also open on a drop-in basis on certain specified days, so check the website before visiting | **Tip** Somewhat tucked away is the Fellows' Garden, in the north-west corner of which can be found the tiny Victorian pets' cemetery, which is full of atmosphere. In 2008 Eric Marland carved a new addition in the form of a stone memorial to Miko, the Master's cat.

83__ The Pint Shop

When Tom met Jerry

Pubs come, pubs go, but these days they mostly go – at the alarming rate of around 20 a week in the UK. So it was heartening to see a brand new pub open in 2013, the first in Cambridge for many years. The owners, Rich and Bennie, spotted an empty office building on Peas Hill, an area once full of nondescript council offices and banks that has since been transformed into one of the most vibrant corners of the city for eating and drinking.

From the outside, the Pint Shop still looks more like the offices it once was than a traditional pub, and there are only discreet signs to give a clue to what lies within: 'MEAT. BREAD. BEER.' The pub reimagines a beer house or 'Tom and Jerry' house, drinking establishments that sprang up in the wake of the 1830 Beer House Act. The government was keen to encourage beer-drinking over spirits, especially gin, which they believed had a detrimental effect on the morals of the working classes. They abolished the tax on beer and introduced establishments that could sell *only* beer. For a modest fee anyone could brew it and sell it.

The Pint Shop décor is a happy mix of semi-rustic furnishings, solid parquet flooring, cool grey-green woodwork and industrial lighting. It all blends together to create a warm and comfortable atmosphere, accommodating ladies who lunch as effortlessly as blokes who want beer. And beer is something that the Pint Shop does supremely well: the blackboard shows 23 different craft ales, ranging from a Nene Valley Bitter at a modest 3.8% abv, to a Dutch Stout of an eye-watering 11.8% abv that is only sold in half-pint measures. The bar snacks are decidedly meaty, but the restaurant has a wide range of good-quality British food that should satisfy all tastes.

And as for spirits, the worthies who passed the Beer House Act would definitely not approve of the 130 sorts of gin that are now available.

Address 10 Peas Hill, CB2 3PP, +44 (0)1223 981070, www.pintshop.co.uk | Getting there Any Citi bus (1–8) to town centre; Grand Arcade car park | Hours Bar Sun–Thu noon–11pm, Fri & Sat noon–midnight; restaurant Sun–Thu noon–9pm, Fri & Sat noon–9.45pm | Tip Hidden away in St Edward's Passage, opposite the bookshop G. David, is the tiny, attractive church of St Edward King and Martyr, some parts of which date back to around 1400. St Edward's, often referred to as 'Teddy's', played a central role in the early days of the Protestant Reformation.

84_ The Pitt Club
Drinking and diving

Britain's youngest ever prime minister, William Pitt the Younger, came to office at the age of 24. The club that bears his name was founded as a political club in 1835 to 'do honour to the name and memory of Mr William Pitt', and uphold the Conservative principles for which he stood. There was a bit of socialising, drinking, toasting and fine dining as well, and it wasn't long before politics was left behind and what endured was a club for undergraduate students. Today it remains a social club, exclusively for students at the University (female students having finally been admitted in 2017).

Until it took up its current premises in 1866 the club was fairly peripatetic, occupying a number of premises in central Cambridge – all of them a good deal more modest than its eventual home. The Hoop Inn in Jesus Lane had been an important coaching inn, but with the coming of the railways its business had begun to dwindle. The site was bought by the Roman Bath Co. Ltd for the erection of Cambridge's first Turkish baths – strangely, with a Roman theme. There was to be a swimming pool and plunge pool, but it would be very unlike a steamy hammam. With a stunning classical portico, the building encapsulated everything in line with the great classical revival so popular at the time.

It seems Cambridge just wasn't ready for Turkish or even Roman baths. They opened in February 1863 and closed just 10 months later. The building was auctioned and bought by the original architect, Sir Matthew Digby Wyatt, who leased it partly to the Pitt Club and partly to Orme's Billiard Rooms. Eventually, in 1907, the Club was able to buy the entire building.

Today, although the ground floor is now occupied by Japanese restaurant Kibou, much of the original building is still recognisable. The pool has been covered over and is now the main dining room, but you can still see the decorative metal grille that used to cover the warm air ducts.

Address 7a Jesus Lane, CB5 8BA, (Kibou) +44 (0)1223 650866, www.kibou.co.uk | **Getting there** City 2 to Jesus Lane; Grand Arcade car park | **Hours** Mon–Sat noon–11pm, Sun noon–10pm | **Tip** At 16 Jesus Lane is the Grade I listed Little Trinity, built around 1725, and probably one of the finest domestic buildings in Cambridge.

85 The Polar Museum

In the footsteps of heroes

It is now over 100 years since the doomed expedition of Captain Robert Falcon Scott to the South Pole ended in tragedy. His party had been trying to retrace their steps across 800 miles of cruel and inhospitable solid ice terrain. On 16 March 1912 Lawrence Oates walked out of the tent, declaring, 'I am just going outside and may be some time.' He was never seen again. Scott, Wilson and Bowers struggled on for nine more days, but the intense cold and lack of food caused them to succumb – just 11 miles away from their food depot.

Many people will know something of the tragic expedition led by Scott, but a visit to the Polar Museum provides a huge amount of detail on the party's movements, through photographs, letters, journals and the wealth of everyday items used on the trip. Displays of scientific instruments, arctic clothing, equipment of the period (Oates' sleeping bag is there) and items of food, including ships' biscuits, mustard and even tobacco pipes, bring the whole era to life.

There are also examples of the local Inuit culture and handicrafts, clothing and methods of transport. Sadly, if there had been a greater rapport with indigenous peoples the outcome of Scott's expedition, and others before it, might have been different. Although Scott's is perhaps the best known, expeditions to the Antarctic to find trade routes had begun as far back as 1670.

In the Arctic Circle, serious attempts to find the Northwest Passage had begun in earnest in 1818 by John Ross, but foundered because of his belief that it was blocked by mountains. In the 1820s William Edward Parry also went in search of the Northwest Passage but was unsuccessful, as was John Franklin, most of whose party died. Among all the doom and failure, the success of the expeditions led by Ernest Shackleton stand out for their heroism and organisational brilliance.

Address Lensfield Road, CB2 1ER, +44 (0)1223 336540, www.spri.cam.ac.uk | Getting there Citi 1, 3, X 3 or 13; Queen Anne Terrace car park | Hours Tue – Sat 10am – 4pm | Tip Housed in a former factory and overlooking Parker's Piece, the Grain and Hop Store in Regent Terrace is a great place to try some cask ales and craft beers, including a special unpasteurised Pilsner Urquell tank beer.

86__Polonia Club

A small slice of Poland in Cambridge

In common with many cities in the UK, Cambridge has experienced an influx of workers from Poland in recent years, but the city's association with that country has a history that dates back to the end of World War II. Brave Polish soldiers and airmen fought alongside British forces, and after the war many found themselves in resettlement camps, prevented from returning home to a country that had now been taken over by the Soviets.

By 1948 there was a sizeable Polish community in Cambridge, who met regularly to socialise and to keep their traditions alive. In 1960 they started to look for their own premises but it was not until 1972, when 250 families jointly took out a loan, that they were able to realise their dream and Polonia was bought. It now houses several meeting rooms, a chapel (with resident priest) where mass is celebrated every day, a library and a restaurant. A low point came in 2007 when customers for the restaurant had dwindled, but when Sylwester Iwaniec spotted an announcement in his church paper he seized the opportunity offered to revive the business.

Polonia's restaurant continues to thrive, now under the careful eye of new owner Monkia Kwiatkowska, who oversees the excellent and authentic cooking. The rustic décor is decidedly Polish and gives the feeling of being in somebody's home. To drink, there are over 60 flavoured vodkas and some well-chosen regional beers from small independent breweries.

The food is not fine dining, but hearty and sustaining: *bigos* (a stew of pork and sauerkraut), *pierogi* (stuffed dumplings) and *placki ziemniaczane* (potato pancakes) are particular specialities, and there is a wide choice of vegetable side dishes and salads. It won't be easy, but do try to leave room for one of the desserts, such as *sernik wiedeński* (cheesecake) or *Wuzetka*, the chocolate cream cake that's often just called WZ. Delicious, or *Pyszne!* as they say.

Address 231 Chesterton Road, CB4 1AS, +44 (0)1223 365854, www.thepolishrestaurant.co.uk | **Getting there** Bus 117 or Citi 2 to Chesterton Road | **Hours** Wed–Sat noon–10pm, Sun noon–8pm | **Tip** There is a place of pilgrimage at nearby 3 Humberstone Road. It's the house where the name 'Pakistan' was first coined in 1933 by its then occupant, Choudhry Rahmat Ali, in his pamphlet the 'Pakistan Declaration'.

87__The Press Museum

The very human side of the world's oldest press

The long, brightly lit corridors leading from the reception area to the Cambridge University Press Museum are enlivened with large framed posters of the alphabets created by David Kindersley (see ch. 104). His association with Cambridge University Press dated back to the 1940s and a meeting with the then University Printer, Brooke Crutchley.

The whole history of the Press is encapsulated in this small, attractive museum. Illustrations, photographs and interesting artefacts show the Press's previous homes, starting with the origins of printing in Cambridge in Free School Lane, through the commissioning of the Pitt Building in Trumpington Street (the commemorative trowel used to lay the first stone in 1831 is there), the London headquarters Bentley House in 1938, the New Printing House in 1963, and in 1981 the Edinburgh Building, which is now the site of the new Cambridge University Press & Assessment offices.

Alongside a reconstruction of an editor's office, with desks free of all technology and displaying a copy of a letter from Albert Einstein to the Press, there are original and facsimile copies of many of the Press's most notable books. Highlights include John Baskerville's Folio Bible of 1763, said to be one of the finest books ever to have been printed in Britain, and facsimiles of John Milton's *Lycidas* of 1638, with his personal annotations, and Isaac Newton's *Principia Mathematica*, one of the seminal works in the history of science.

More everyday displays, many donated by former employees, are just as interesting and provide an insight into the arcane world of printing and publishing. There are compositors' tools, a monotype machine for producing hot metal type, a riposte to a complaint about the introduction of steam presses in 1839, and stern notices regarding the length of tea breaks. You will even discover how printers enjoyed a 'wayzgoose' each year.

Address Cambridge University Press & Assessment, University Printing House, Shaftesbury Road, CB2 8EA, +44 (0)1223 553311, www.cambridge.org | **Getting there** The Universal buses stop at Hills Road and Brooklands Avenue | **Hours** By appointment only; contact archivespress@cambridge.org to arrange a visit | **Tip** The Hills Road Sports and Tennis Centre in nearby Purbeck Road (www.hillsroadsportscentre.co.uk) is open to all. As well as all the usual racquet sports, the Centre offers cricket practice, Pilates classes, kettlebell, a fully-equipped fitness suite and a therapy room.

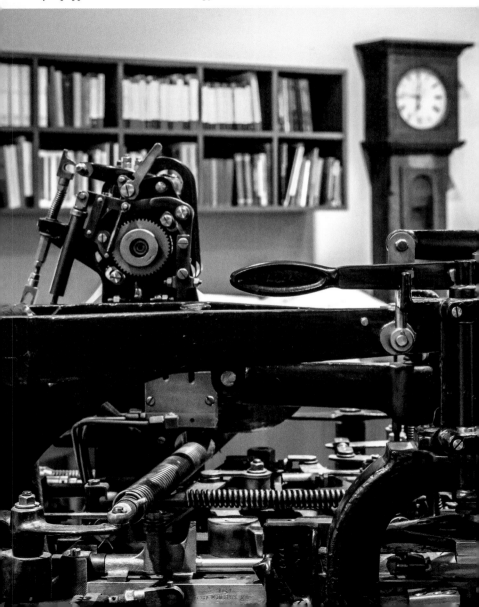

88_ Queens' College Sundial

Casting a shadow in Old Court

Whoever conceived of the idea of a sundial that would also act as a moondial must have been a supreme optimist. When the sun shone, the 'style' (the bar that projects from the face of the dial) cast a shadow that pointed to the correct position on the face. So far so good, on cloudless days at least. However, when it came to the moondial, not only did it need to be a clear sky, but it was only accurate on the night of a full moon: after that, the moondial lost time every night and was over five hours out after only a week. Nevertheless, this failed to discourage moondial enthusiasts, who compiled intricate charts to correct for this.

The Queens' College sundial is among the most remarkable in the world, being celebrated for its colourful motifs and the intricacy of its design. Not only does the sundial tell the hours of the day in Roman numerals, but it also shows the months in Latin, the signs of the zodiac, the time of sunrise and the hours of daylight. To enable it to be used as a moondial there is a table underneath that gives the moon's hour angle for every day of the lunar cycle. Such tables can also be used as predictors of the tide, but in landlocked Cambridge they have been somewhat underused.

The sundial was first constructed in 1642 and is often attributed to Isaac Newton – erroneously, since he was only born in that year. It acquired its current decoration in 1733, fell into decay and by 1860 had lost its gnomon and all its remaining ironwork. It has been repainted five times since 1911, most recently in 1971. In 1968, the clunch stone backing on which the paint was applied was found to be unstable, so the sundial was rendered with cement and repainted, an operation that led to all manner of errors being introduced. The rendering degenerated very quickly and it all had to be completely redone. Fortunately, later repainting has corrected some of these earlier errors.

Address Silver Street, CB3 9ET, +44 (0)1223 335511, www.queens.cam.ac.uk | **Getting there** Any Citi bus (1–8) to town centre; some pay and display parking along Queens' Road, otherwise Grand Arcade car park | **Hours** Daily 10am–4pm. College closed during exam periods; contact Porters' Lodge to check | **Tip** Be sure to cross over the famous Mathematical Bridge that connects the two parts of Queens' College, and then stroll along the Backs up to the very steep Garret Hostel Bridge, which will take you back to the centre of town. Watch out for cyclists, as they come by at breakneck speed.

89_Real Tennis Club

More fun than Quidditch

A real tennis court looks like a bizarre cross between a Mondrian canvas and a motorway flyover. No part of it is symmetrical, and the naming of parts is highly eccentric: there are hazards, galleries and penthouses – but the galleries are on the floor. The net droops in the middle, and you score by whacking balls against a red square or through holes in the wall, making a bell ring. The rules sound as though they're made up as you go along and the handicap system requires complex pre-match calculations. The yellow balls are hard, not bouncy, and move at 100 mph, enough to knock an unwary photographer off his feet.

'Real' is a corruption of 'royal' and indicates the traditionally elevated status of most players since the sport was first established in the 16th century. Most real tennis courts are found in clubs, stately homes, private schools and universities. There are an estimated 10,000 regular players worldwide, more than half of whom are in the UK. However, real tennis is growing and increasingly democratised, limited only by the number of accessible courts.

The University Real Tennis Club is one of only four clubs in the world with two courts. The older of the two is world-class, demonstrated by the patina on the floor and walls: for *aficionados* of the sport, the sheer grey wall is a thing of beauty. Although it is a University sports club, it has a large proportion of non-University members and a substantial number of women and junior players. About a third of the membership are beginners but three of the four semi-finalists in the 2016 Amateur Championship were members of the club.

The club welcomes spectators and visitors – just contact the club to check someone is available to show you round – and is always pleased to see would-be members. If you are lucky enough to see a match, stand well back from the netting – it's there for a very good reason.

Address 56 Grange Road, CB3 9DJ, www.curtc.net, +44 (0)1223 357106 | Getting there Bus 18 or 75 (75 not Sun) to Newnham opposite Grange Road | Hours Mon–Fri 9am–5pm, Sat 9am–noon | Tip The honours boards alongside the Blue Court list the winners of club competitions. One of the earliest champions (1909) was G. H. Hardy, the mathematician and scientist portrayed by Jeremy Irons in *The Man Who Knew Infinity*, which also starred Dev Patel as Srinivasa Ramanujan. The opening scenes of the film were shot on the Blue Court.

90 __ Reality Checkpoint

Where gown and town part company

How can an apparently ordinary lamp post have been designated a Grade II listed building and become such an icon for Cambridge residents?

Bang in the middle of the two paths that bisect the green space known as Parker's Piece stands a large cast-iron lamp post, believed to be the oldest electrical lamp post in the city, on which the words 'Reality Checkpoint' were scratched over 40 years ago. The lamp post, which was installed around 1860 as a gas light and later converted to electricity, sits on a large square plinth and is painted a tasteful verdigris shade, decorated with scrolled wrought-iron, writhing dolphins and red and white stylised flowers. American GIs celebrating the end of the war with Japan are reported to have torn down the lamp post above the dolphins, but in 1947 it was repaired and the single lamp replaced by four, which is how it remains today, casting its watery light over the centre of the park.

For the majority of Cambridge students, Parker's Piece is at the outer limits of their perception of Cambridge – any further out towards Mill Road starts to become dangerously uncharted territory. So the lamp post has been claimed to be the place where the student part of the city ends and the real world begins.

Reality Checkpoint acquired its arresting name in the 1970s when, the story goes, students from Cambridge Art School (now part of Anglia Ruskin University) painted on the words under the guidance of one of their tutors. For a brief moment in 1998, the lamp post carried a plaque bearing its name, but as it was only attached with superglue it wasn't long before this vanished. Since then the lettering has been repainted many times, and painted out just as often by the council. The lamp post has recently been lovingly restored, showing off its many special features. Look out for the tiny door at its base, inviting people to check reality themselves.

Address Parker's Piece, CB1 1PN | Getting there Any bus to Drummer Street Bus Station; Queen Anne Terrace car park | Tip Cross over Parkside and stroll past some of Cambridge's most attractive terraced houses in Melbourne Place, Warkworth Street and Eden Street. End your walk with a drink at the Elm Tree.

91 Relevant Record Café

It's not just nostalgia

What is it about vinyl that has led to its huge comeback? Andy Powell, who runs the record side of this independent record store, will tell you that it's the warmth, texture and depth of sound that analogue gives you – something that just can't be matched by music that has been compressed digitally. Then there's the aesthetic appeal of the record sleeve, the tactile experience of sorting through the covers, slipping the record out of its sleeve and placing it on the turntable.

When the shop opened, its second-hand records were largely Andy's own. Customers began to come in, curious to know if their grandparents' jazz collection might be valuable, so the staff had to develop a feel for what to buy and how much to spend on it. Now they stock over 5,000 records, of which about a third are second-hand, and their range is constantly expanding to cater for their loyal regulars. They have the largest selection of new vinyl in Cambridge. Anything really rare will quickly get scooped up by knowledgeable browsers, who often call by once or twice a week. And everyone who works in the shop is a vinyl fan, so naturally whenever they are out and about they scour charity shops and vintage stores for that elusive rarity to bring back.

The café is Angie Powell's realm, and together with her friendly team she has created a real community centre with good coffee at its heart. This is made from the finest, ethically sourced Arabica beans, but tea lovers won't be disappointed, as the tea is loose and served in pots. The background music is excellent (as you'd expect), interesting artwork covers the walls, and the tables, chairs and china are all mismatched, which makes for a cosy, cheerful atmosphere. Many regulars visit every day for breakfast, and the brunch is especially popular. Other favourites are the home-made cakes (including gluten-free), salads and sausage rolls.

Address 260 Mill Road, CB1 3NF, +44 (0)1223 244684, www.relevantrecordcafe.co.uk |
Getting there Citi 2 to Romsey Terrace | **Hours** Records: daily 10am–5pm, café
9am–5pm | **Tip** Coleridge Recreation Ground has some state-of-the-art play equipment
for children that is the first of its kind in the UK. The stars of the show are the slide that
comes out of a huge fierce dragon's mouth, and the splashpads. For adults, there are facilities
for football, tennis and table tennis.

92 Riverboat Rosie

Messing about on the river

There can be few better ways of slowing down the pace than drifting down the river while someone else does all the hard work.

The Rosie, a passenger narrowboat that was once used to raise funds for a charity in the Midlands, became derelict and was acquired for restoration and brought to Cambridge. Once there, her owner started to use her for river trips. A few years ago, Peter Watson and family took over the business, and have been steadily expanding it.

The Rosie's companion vessel is the eco-friendly electric boat the Princess Charlotte (named following an open competition). Both can take up to 12 passengers, but if you turn up on your own or with just a friend, you'll still get the trip (and the guide).

The east bank of the Cam is home to a community of houseboats, while on the west bank are all the college boathouses. You might spot a cormorant, holding its wings out to dry, a family of swans in no hurry to move out of the way of the boats, some of the keen anglers who regularly catch pike, eels and chub, and almost certainly a boat crew out practising. Midsummer Common gives way to Riverside, once the scene of great commercial activity where boats would dock and cargos were delivered. Travelling at a gentle three to four miles an hour, you will pass the old Cambridge Pumping Station where some extended trips will cruise past Stourbridge Common, the site of the largest medieval fair in the country, and still grazed by cattle today. Chesterton appears on the west bank before the countryside opens up and you reach the city boundary and the village of Fen Ditton, a picturesque village whose name means 'the village by the ditch' and is associated with the annual college rowing races known as The Bumps. There you can stop for a drink and wait for the boat to slowly turn round and return you to the noise and bustle of the real world.

Address By Jesus Lock, Chesterton Road, CB4 3BD, +44 (0)7706 734763, www.camboats.co.uk | **Getting there** Citi 2 to Jesus Green | **Hours** See website for cruising times | **Tip** Just over the other side of the bridge on Jesus Green are a table-tennis table and six outdoor tennis courts. They are all free to use on a first-come, first-served basis.

93___School of Pythagoras

A small slice of Oxford in Cambridge

The handsome stone building with the curious name of the School of Pythagoras, which stands in the grounds of St John's College, was constructed around the mid-12th century and is one of the oldest buildings in Cambridge. Originally called the Stone House, it belonged to the Dunning family. Eustace Dunning, a man of considerable wealth, occupied the house with his wife and three children. Records show that his grandson Hervey Fitz Eustace, an alderman who was elected mayor of Cambridge in 1207, later also lived at this house.

By 1270 the Dunning family's wealth had declined appreciably and the house had to be sold, and so after 100 years of family ownership, it went to one Walter de Merton. The Merton family was from Oxford and Walter de Merton, Lord Chancellor to Henry III and founder of Merton College, used the new acquisition to house students from Oxford who were fleeing persecution and civil unrest in that city. If Merton's intention was to create a *domus scholarium* it was short-lived because in 1277, after Merton's death, the home was managed by a succession of bailiffs and tenant farmers engaged by Merton College.

As is to be expected with a building of this age, it has been put to many different uses over the centuries. It was certainly used as a hostel for students of law and mathematics, which may explain the link to Pythagoras, although nobody knows for sure how that came about. It has also been a boarding school, and at one point accommodated women attending lectures in the days before Newnham College was fully established. It was even rented after World War II by Lord Rothschild, a former MI5 agent and think-tank head. In 1959 the building was bought by St John's for use as a drama studio and lecture theatre. Finally, in modern times, and after undergoing extensive sympathetic renovation, it has become an archive centre for the college.

Address St John's College, St John's Street, CB2 1TP, +44 (0)1223 338600,
www.joh.cam.ac.uk | **Getting there** Any Citi bus (1–8) to town centre; Grand Arcade car
park. It is slightly tricky to find inside the college, so be persistent! | **Hours** Wed & Thu
9.30am–4pm, by appointment only; contact archivist@joh.cam.ac.uk to book. Otherwise
viewable from the outside during college opening hours | **Tip** Opposite St John's is
Le Patissier, a small, welcoming café with plenty of seating (and umbrellas!) outside, so you
can relax and take in the beautiful architecture all around you.

94_ Sedgwick Museum of Earth Sciences

A jaw-dropping tour of our history

The Sedgwick Museum is a splendid example of late Victorian architecture, with high ceilings, tall windows, polished wood and glass-fronted cabinets crammed with fossils. Many exhibits have the original exquisite handwritten labels. It has just two-and-a-bit L-shaped rooms, but every bay contains treasures to amaze and perplex, from shells smaller than the smallest fingernail to the skull of a *Tyrannosaurus rex*, whose huge maw is the first thing you see when you enter.

When Stan, the *T. rex*, was first repositioned at the museum entrance, there was concern that he would frighten visiting children. But they seem to take Stan in their stride, along with the interactive displays, quizzes, books and activities that are child-level features of the main rooms.

Starting at the heyday of Victorian acquisition following the museum's founding a century earlier, you go back in time over 500 million years to the earliest evidence of abundant life on Earth. As a student of the University, Darwin features largely, as a geologist rather than evolutionary scientist. Stepping back from him, you discover that hippos once lumbered across Cambridgeshire, that the fossils of starfish, algae and leaves are startlingly like the forms we see today, and that the Himalayas were once over five miles below the sea.

The museum displays just a fraction of the collection's 2.5 million specimens, of which nearly 10,000 were bequeathed to the University by John Woodward in the early 18th century. This collection was built on by Professor Adam Sedgwick, after whom the museum is named. Display cases feature donations from professional and amateur collectors, including Alfred, Lord Tennyson. The museum continues to be a research and teaching centre, in the spirit in which it was founded.

Address Downing Street, CB2 3EQ, +44 (0)1223 333456, www.sedgwickmuseum.org | Getting there Any Citi bus (1–8) to town centre; Grand Arcade car park | Hours Mon–Fri 10am–5pm, Sat 10am–4pm | Tip If you fancy lunch or tea after your visit, Trockel, Ulmann & Freunde, known as the German café, in nearby Pembroke Street, serves inexpensive soups, sandwiches and cakes. It is very popular with students.

95__Shakespeare Festival
Helping to keep the Bard real

Those people you see in Elizabethan costume in the streets of Cambridge during July and August are promoting the annual Shakespeare Festival. Every year the company puts on eight plays selected from the complete works – comedies, histories and tragedies – and for eight summer weeks these are performed in the gardens of several Cambridge colleges.

The festival was started in 1988 with very few resources. In the early years, the artistic director, David Crilly, struggled to meet the cost of costume hire and to convince the colleges that they could safely open their gardens to players and audiences during the height of the holiday season. Now the festival is a highlight in the city's calendar and the company is thriving.

You will not find any gimmicky staging in these performances – no quasi-Soviet imagery, motorbikes, machine-guns or palaces presented as boardrooms. The gardens provide the sets for all the plays, there are no stages, props are minimal, and costumes traditional. Productions are never repeated, so even the most popular plays, which appear regularly in the festival programme, are always new productions with new actors and directors. The gardens open in time for pre-performance picnics and the evening becomes increasingly magical as the light and sounds from outside fade away. One of the most appealing aspects of the festival is the chance to visit gardens that remain private for the rest of the year and are at their most beautiful during the summer months.

It is usual to bring a picnic supper, and the pre-performance period can be very convivial. Seating is provided, although some of the audience prefer to bring rugs and enjoy the evening more informally. Rain, in an English summer, is always a possibility, but even if the weather looks dodgy the show will go on. As David Crilly says 'only the most biblical of downpours' will end a performance.

Address See www.cambridgeshakespeare.com for programme and details of venues |
Getting there See website for details | **Hours** July & Aug; college gardens open at 6.30pm |
Tip Even on the most beautiful day the gardens can become chilly when the sun goes down.
Bring a rug or something warm to wear, and don't forget the mosquito repellent. If rain is
expected, come armed with umbrellas and something waterproof.

96__Snowy Farr Statue

'I believe in giving not receiving'

Newly arrived residents and visitors to Cambridge could be forgiven for being puzzled by the rather comical statue that stands outside the Guildhall. Whether it is a fitting tribute to eccentric fundraiser Walter 'Snowy' Farr has been hotly debated since the statue was unveiled in 2012.

Snowy Farr, born in 1919, was one of the last of the county council's roadmen. When he retired he began to spend his weekends collecting money for his chosen charities. His love of dressing up, together with his brilliantly decorated tricycle (bearing the words GODISLOVE, SNOWYKING and NEWWORLD SMILE) and an entourage of small animals, made him a focal point for anyone visiting the Market Square. He would often be seen, his cheeks brightly rouged, wearing a black top hat, red military jacket, white jodhpurs and black striped boots – although he had quite an extensive range of other colourful outfits. White mice would run around the brim of his hat or down into the bushy beard he cultivated specially for them to scamper through. He trained a series of white cats to sit on his hat, each one staying there for just 10 minutes before another took over the job.

Over many decades Snowy raised a total of £125,000 for a variety of charities, and in 1995 he was awarded the MBE in recognition of his work. Characteristically modest, Snowy summed up his philosophy by saying that he had been 'helped by God to help others'.

When Snowy died in 2007, a campaign was started to produce a memorial to this much-loved local character. The city council held an open competition, and British sculptor Gary Webb's vibrant abstract work was chosen. The ten-foot-high statue now stands outside the Guildhall where Snowy spent so much time collecting money. It is obviously popular with children, who enjoy clambering over its base, and with the city's many buskers, who often set up just in front of it.

Address Market Square, CB2 3QI | Getting there Bus 199 to Bene't Street; Grand Arcade car park | Tip Walk down Guildhall Street towards Fisher House, and glance through the gateway to your left, where you'll see a copy of a beautiful relief by Andrea della Robbia (1435 – 1525).

97__St Bene't's Church

A small church with a prodigious history

St Bene't's is modest to the point of self-effacing. It sits in the middle of Bene't Street, surrounded by eateries, pubs and artisanal shops selling beguiling if non-essential items. All of these are upstarts compared with the little church, which is the oldest in the county and the oldest building in the city. It has stood on this spot for at least 1,000 years, predating the arrival of William the Conqueror and the scholars who founded the University.

Many aspects of the church's original Saxon structure are intact, most obviously the unpretentious, three-stage tower, which houses six bells that are rung weekly. For many years St Bene't's has been firmly linked with the history of change-ringing, as the famous 17th-century campanologist, Fabian Stedman, is believed to have been the parish clerk here. However, this has been somewhat shaken by the discovery that Stedman appears to have been in London at the same time, suggesting that St Bene't's Stedman might be a coincidence rather than the same man.

In 1352 Corpus Christi College, then called Bene't College, was founded and used St Bene't's for over 200 years until the college chapel was completed in 1579. There was a passageway, now blocked off, leading from the college into the church. Other changes have been made over time, including the delightful painted ceilings, which are decorated with golden angels and crowned figures.

The church houses some interesting religious and secular artefacts, all explained in the simple but informative guide available in the church for a small donation. Of particular note is the 18th-century memorial to John Randall, the University's professor of music, of whom it says, 'The Sweetness of his Harmonies charmed the Ear, and the Mildness of his Manners the Heart.' The tributes to his wife ('a Woman of exemplary Piety and discretion!') and daughter-in-law are equally touching.

Address Bene't St, CB2 3PT, www.stbenetschurch.org | **Getting there** Any Citi bus (1–8) to town centre; Grand Arcade car park | **Hours** Daily 9am–6.30pm, but closed Thu 10am–noon | **Tip** Down Bene't Street opposite the Corn Exchange is Aromi, a genuine Sicilian café, where a queue forms outside from early lunchtime for their pizza slices, focaccia and other hot dishes. A second branch just around the corner on Peas Hill serves delicious home-made gelato.

98 St Botolph's Church
The Darwin family church

Botwulf of Thorney, also called Botulf, Botulph or Botolph, was an East Anglian abbot and a patron saint of travellers. His name inspired the naming of Boston in Lincolnshire (Botolph's Town), which in turn gave its name to Boston in Massachusetts.

St Botolph's church was built in 1350 on the site of earlier Saxon and Norman churches. It stands on the site of Trumpington Gate, the old medieval southern gateway to the city; before a journey was undertaken, prayers would have been said at the church, and thanks given after a safe return. A south porch and south chapel were added to the original church in the mid-15th century, and in 1872 the chancel was rebuilt by G. F. Bodley, the great architect of the English Gothic Revival period. On the hexagonal buttress of the clock tower's south-west corner is a pair of identical sundials – undoubtedly of great use to all those early travellers.

Inside, the church is quietly elegant and tranquil, offering sanctuary from the bustle of King's Parade. By the vestry door is a memorial to Charles Darwin's grandson, Charles Galton Darwin: the family were parishioners of St Botolph's. Further memorials commemorate the generosity of other parishioners to the church and to the poor, and if you look carefully you will see the ancient black parish chest that once held the donations. Close by is the font with its 17th-century Laudian canopy – an octagonal confection of columns, ornamental shields and carved roses, all crowned by an acorn.

Screened off from the rest of the church, and usually kept locked, is a memorial chapel to those who died in World War I. On the west wall of the chapel you can see the colourful and mysterious half-length effigy of Thomas Playfere, the eminent 16th-century professor of divinity, erected by his widow, Alicia, who also commissioned the rather extravagant inscription to his memory that appears below the figure.

Address Trumpington Street, CB2 1RG, +44 (0)1223 351326, www.stbotolphcam.org |
Getting there Any Citi bus (1–8) to town centre; Grand Arcade car park | Hours Daily
9am–4.30pm; see website for times of services | Tip Follow Botolph Lane (known in
the 16th century as Penny Farthing Lane) into Free School Lane where, on the façade of
the original Cavendish Laboratory, is Eric Gill's *Cavendish Crocodile*, carved in *sgraffito* in
memory of the laboratory's director Ernest Rutherford, who was nicknamed 'the Crocodile'
by fellow physicist Piotr Kapitza.

99 St Clement's Church

The oldest church in 'Bridgeland'

In a city with an embarrassment of churches, it is sad but perhaps not surprising that the congregation of St Clement's has dwindled in recent years. And yet the church carries on with its loyal followers, who look after the building and are determined to keep it open for Christian worship and not allow it to go the way of so many other Cambridge churches that have closed or been repurposed. It has been in a bad state of disrepair, and is a little gloomy inside, but thanks to a grant it has recently been restored and is now open to the public once more.

St Clement's is right on the street in a rather cramped site between Thompson's Lane and Portugal Place, in the heart of what was once medieval Cambridge. The churchyard at the back is tiny and full of wild flowers, and there is a very unusual iconographic monument to a past vicar of the church, Canon Edmund Gough de Salis Wood, who came in 1865 and stayed for a remarkable 65 years.

The core of the building – the doorway and nave – dates back to the 13th century, making it one of the oldest in the city, but it has been greatly modified over time. During the 16th century the aisles were widened and the chancel rebuilt. The tower, built in 1821 and apparently inserted between old aisles, was described by Nikolaus Pevsner as 'somewhat silly'. It once had a spire but this was removed in 1928.

The jewel in the crown of St Clement's is the magnificent mural on the east wall behind the altar, which shows Christ in majesty surrounded by saints and angels. It was painted in 1872 by the workshop of Cambridge's 'master artworkman' Frederick Leach, and equals anything he painted in nearby All Saints' Church.

As you leave by the west door, leaning against the wall is a grim reminder of the transience of life. Here, on a grave slab, is the grinning figure of Death, holding in one hand a spear and in the other an hourglass.

Address Bridge Street, CB2 1UF, www.stclementscambridge.co.uk | Getting there Citi 2 to Bridge Street; Grand Arcade car park | Hours Mon–Fri 11.45am–2.30pm, Sun 10.15am–1.30pm; check website for details of the lunchtime recitals | Tip Portugal Place is a fine example of mainly 19th-century townhouses. Number 19–20, named the Golden Helix, was once the home of Francis Crick, who along with James Watson discovered DNA (look out for the double helix above the front door). An ancient pear tree grows in a tiny, pretty oasis of vegetation in front of the house.

100 St Ives

How many going to St Ives?

As rocketing property prices in Cambridge drive buyers further from the city, the delightful market town of St Ives seems to be in a strange but encouraging state of arrested decline. Beautifully converted old properties now rub shoulders with modern developments and new businesses attract more and more people to the place. Whether or not you are house hunting, this little gem of a town is within easy reach of Cambridge via The Busway (see ch. 17) and has everything you need for a perfect day out – a river, many cafés, pubs and restaurants, and plenty of history.

Start with a stroll along The Pavement, perhaps stopping for a coffee at Di Rita's (converted from an old bank) where you can plan your itinerary and view the statue of Oliver Cromwell, looking every inch the leader, despite the fact that St Ives was Cromwell's home at a particularly low period of his life, when he struggled with poverty and poor mental health. Continue onto The Broadway and drop into the Norris Museum to learn more about the town's history and examine more Cromwelliana before turning back towards the quay. Floods Tavern is the ideal place to pause for a glass of chilled white wine and watch the boats and ducks on the river. At the quayside, you could take a boat trip, enjoy lunch at Amore and wander across the old bridge, which incorporates a chapel (a very rare feature).

From here you can follow an undemanding circular walk of five miles via the Hemingfords to Houghton Mill, a working watermill, owned by the National Trust. The riverside path returns you to St Ives through the churchyard, which lost its spire in World War I when struck by a plane, an accident in which the trainee pilot also lost his life. After this, you will feel you've earned a delicious cake at the Commute café before heading home, not having met a single man with any number of wives, sacks, cats or kits.

Getting there The Busway (see www.thebusway.info); by car via A14/A1307/A1096 | **Hours**
Market days: Monday (8.30am–3pm) and Friday (8.30am–2pm) | **Tip** The Manor at
Hemingford Grey, just over a mile from St Ives, was the home of novelist Lucy Boston, who
renamed it 'Green Knowe' in her famous children's stories. Both house and garden are open
throughout the year but you will need to make an appointment to visit the house. For entry
fees and more details go to www.greenknowe.co.uk.

101 Stapleford Granary

A state-of-the art home for the arts

Tucked away in the village of Stapleford, four miles south of Cambridge, is the Granary. Considered state-of-the-art when it was built in the late 19th century, this handsome building is now a lively centre for the arts, attracting top-flight performers and artists, and has a highly popular café that is open six days a week. It is fast developing a nationwide reputation for the events and activities it hosts and from an annual footfall of 8,000 in 2019 can now boast more than 60,000 visitors a year, both local and from much further afield.

The conversion of the Granary's buildings won a regional RIBA award in 2019. The work involved rebuilding tumbledown structures, reusing existing materials as far as possible and developing sympathetically. The design provides flow, light and discrete gallery and exhibition spaces while linking all in one whole that offers both stimulation and relaxation. The beautiful concert hall is augmented in the summer months with outdoor concerts in the tented courtyard. There are around 60 classical, folk and jazz concerts a year, children's theatre, and poetry readings.

The centre has a close relationship with the local community. Pupils at Stapleford Primary School visit weekly to take part in a variety of creative activities. Studio spaces can be rented by artists and artisans to work and hold classes, and the Granary also offers unique spaces for conferences with a range of hospitality packages.

Most visitors will want to spend time in the café, which has a range of seating areas, from a cosy poetry corner to an outdoor area for visitors with dogs, and serves excellent coffee, delicious cakes and light lunches. A recent innovation is the opening of the brook-side orchard behind the Granary, with picnic benches and a converted horsebox selling hot and cold drinks, cake and ice creams. Something for everyone, of all ages.

Address Bury Road, Stapleford, CB22 5BP, +44 (0)1223 849004,
www.staplefordgranary.org.uk | Getting there A1307; Citi7 bus to London Road; 7a
and 31 bus to Bury Road (Poplar Way). Wheelchair access to all areas of the site | Hours
Mon & Tue 8.30am–4pm, Thu & Fri 8.30am–4pm, Sat 9am–3pm, Sun 10am–3pm | Tip
The many times great-grandfather of President Barack Obama, Thomas Blossom, lived in
Stapleford before sailing to America on the second *Mayflower*. The Blossom family graves
are in the churchyard of St Mary the Virgin, now sadly unmarked, but the 600-year-old
church is well worth a visit.

102_ Stir

A real community hub

Opening a new café on the corner of a noisy and busy main road that is also outside the city centre and in a predominantly residential area might not seem the wisest or most promising business decision. However, the confident and imaginative Judith and Matt Harrison saw the potential of a former grocery store, and from the day it opened Stir was a real part of the local community.

The décor is a vibrant coming together of Nordic and industrial styles, in restful shades of grey and white with funky lighting. A bar and high stools along the front window cater for some of the many freelancers who drop in for breakfast or coffee. There's plenty of space inside, too, with seating for about 100 at attractive and comfortable tables, and another 40 seats outside in a pleasant space that's been created out of the pavement area. On warm days it's a suntrap, but on cooler days you will find a basket of cosy rugs to keep you warm. It's the perfect place to sit if you want to unwind with a newspaper or a good book. Young mothers and small children gather at lunchtime. Office workers come along for meetings and breaks, and large tables are provided for the rowing crews who drop in on weekend mornings. A huge blackboard covers one wall, with all the latest menu information. Why not treat yourself to Stir's Big Brunch, accompanied by an Immune Booster Shot or (yes, really) a Beetroot Latte?

Stir offers good coffee, obtained from an award-winning roastery in Brixton, and food that's sourced locally where possible. It's open all day for breakfast, brunch and lunch, with a variety of simple food like soup and sourdough bread (with a good choice of fillings, including vegetarian options) and ultra-healthy salads. The cakes and pastries are first-class too, with several gluten-free options available.

Right next door is the Stir bakery selling artisan breads and pastries you can order online for collection here or in the Green Street shop. And you can now find branches in Fulbourn and Histon.

Address 253 Chesterton Road, CB4 1BG, +44 (0)1223 778530, www.stircambridge.co.uk | Getting there Bus 117 or Citi 2 to Chesterton Road | Hours Mon–Sat 8am–4pm, Sun 9am–4pm | Tip Walk towards Elizabeth Way and there, grand but rather forlorn on the other side of the roundabout, is the 17th-century Chesterton Hall. It was built by Thomas Hobson (of Hobson's choice – 'take it or leave it' – fame) and has now been converted into flats.

103_ Strawberry Fair

The fair that is always a festival

The University may have its May Balls, held confusingly in June of course, but the city has its Strawberry Fair, an extravaganza of stalls, activities, art, cabaret, comedy, dance and music that takes place on the first Saturday in June. Strawberry Fair is a hugely popular event that attracts 30,000 visitors to what is one of the last free festivals in the country and a showcase for local talent. The Fair is well known as a family-friendly event that maintains the atmosphere of a Stonehenge-style hippy fair.

The Fair is run entirely by volunteers, known as the Strawberry Fairies, on a not-for-profit basis, and it is self-funding with no sponsors. Planning for the following year's festival begins almost as soon as the last one has ended. The Strawberry Fairies work through the year to raise funds, run benefit gigs, organise the Cambridge Band Competition and generally help to make sure that it all happens.

The Fair begins with a parade through the city centre, which arrives on Midsummer Common for the grand opening at midday. There are cafés, beer tents selling local ales, stalls selling food from around the world, others selling clothes and plants – and if you want your hair braided or a henna tattoo there is sure to be someone who can help. With 11 stages there is music to suit all tastes and there are also demonstrations of anything from Lindy Hop to tai chi that take place alongside workshops on mindfulness and willow-weaving. The Fair also has a large enclosed children's area that has its own dedicated activities and entertainments.

As the sun goes down (although sun is never guaranteed) and many families head for home, the Fair focuses on music and dance until the grand finale at 10.30pm. After it's all over and the people have left, the Strawberry Fairies set to work clearing everything away so that no one would ever know that the Fair had been there on Midsummer Common, and has done so ever since 1974.

Address Midsummer Common, CB5 8DJ, www.strawberry-fair.org.uk | Getting there
Citi 8 to opposite Jesus College on Victoria Avenue | Hours 10.30am – 11pm | Tip
The other major free community event that takes place on Midsummer Common is the
spectacular firework display, held every 5 November. For safety reasons the organisers ask
that people do not bring their own fireworks or sparklers.

104_ Street Signs

Hidden in plain sight

How do we navigate our way around an unfamiliar place? Now it can all be done via GPS on a mobile phone, but in the past and for those who prefer a more self-reliant approach, street signs giving road names have always been vital. Yet who gives them a second thought?

Someone who gave them more than a second thought was David Kindersley, the letter-carver and typeface-designer whose workshop was in Barton. Walking through Cambridge one day shortly after World War II, Kindersley was appalled to see the cast-iron street names being removed and replaced with new signs using very inferior Ministry of Transport lettering, which he thought was also badly spaced. He set about designing a street name alphabet, one that would have within it the system of spacing that he judged so important – only to have it turned down by Cambridge council. However, it was then chosen by the Ministry of Transport and subsequently selected from a catalogue by Cambridge council, who failed to recognise the typeface they had rejected. In this roundabout way the new Kindersley typeface finally reached Cambridge and other cities across the UK, including London.

When the Grand Arcade was being planned, the developers, Grosvenor Estates, approached the Kindersley workshop (by then run by his widow, Lida Lopes Cardozo) to design a version of the street lettering for use throughout the shopping mall. The original typeface had been chosen by Grosvenor for its elegance and simplicity, but was lacking any lower-case letters or italics, so these needed to be designed. The new alphabet has been called, unsurprisingly, 'Grand Arcade', and is now freely available as a digital typeface. You can see the name across the main entrance in enormous metal letters. At night when the gates are closed the initials 'GA' stand out against the vertical bars that use Kindersley's famous optical letter spacing system.

Address Most of the street names in central Cambridge; Grand Arcade, St Andrew's Street, CB2 3BJ | **Tip** Many of the decorative inscriptions and commemorative plaques seen in the colleges and all around the city are from the Kindersley workshop.

105 __ Trinity College
Secrets and spies

One of the four wealthiest institutions in Britain, Trinity College is the largest college in Cambridge and justifiably flaunts its success. It boasts a stellar list of alumni from its founding in the 16th century to today – poets, novelists, scientists, philosophers and politicians, including 32 Nobel Prize winners and 6 prime ministers. Yet support for the rarefied intellectual atmosphere of the college has some surprising sources. It is less well-known that Trinity owns a substantial area of the container port at Felixstowe, a large share in Tesco real estate and the O2 Arena in London.

Perhaps it is Trinity's ability to be both prominent and inscrutable that has made it a nursery for spies and secret societies. After all, hiding in plain sight is a basic espionage skill. Trinity does not trumpet its association with the Cambridge Five, a group of spies recruited by the KGB when they were students in the 1930s. Four of the five (Anthony Blunt, Kim Philby, John Cairncross and Guy Burgess) were at Trinity; the fifth, Donald Maclean, at Trinity Hall. All held posts in the diplomatic service or British intelligence. Burgess and Maclean defected to the Soviet Union in 1951 and Philby 12 years later. Blunt confessed to the British secret service in 1964 and became an informant. He was publicly exposed in 1979. Cairncross confessed when Burgess and Maclean defected, but he was not revealed as the fifth man until 1990, five years before his death.

Burgess and Blunt were also members of another secret club – the Cambridge Apostles, a self-selecting group of the 12 cleverest undergraduates in the University. Both men were gay and members of the Communist Party, things best kept quiet about at the time. The exposure of the Cambridge Five first brought the Apostles to public attention. The society still exists today, exclusive but no longer clandestine.

Address Trinity College, CB2 1TQ, +44 (0)1223 338400, www.trin.cam.ac.uk | Getting there Any Citi bus (1–8) to town centre; Grand Arcade car park | Hours Daily 10am–5pm; closed last week in Dec until 1 Jan (inclusive); guided tours daily 10am and 2pm | Tip Across the road from the college is Heffers, which has been the University bookshop for nearly a century and a half. Heffers specialises in promoting outstanding non-fiction titles. Its Heffers Choice section is a magnet for regular customers, and the shop is a wonderful place for browsing.

106— The Union

Arguing seriously since 1815

A drunken brawl between college debating societies sounds like an unpromising start to what became The Cambridge Union Society, but from this base a world-class debating society emerged. Its first meeting place was at the Red Lion Inn in Petty Cury, but in 1866 it was able to move to its current building, designed by Alfred Waterhouse.

There is a myth that Hitler undertook not to bomb either Oxford or Cambridge, in return for the Allies sparing the university towns of Heidelberg and Göttingen. Not so. In late July 1942 the area around the Union was attacked by a single low-flying raider armed with explosive incendiary bombs. It caused significant damage to Round Church Street, and shrapnel peppered the walls of Whewell's Court on nearby Jesus Lane. The Union took the force of the blast and a great fire broke out, severely damaging the fabric of the building, including the library (where some of the older books still reveal shrapnel damage) but luckily not the debating chamber, which consequently looks today much as it did in the beginning. The building was fixed up in time to be used as a base from which General Eisenhower and Field Marshal Montgomery planned part of the 1944 Allied invasion of Normandy.

The array of speakers who have passed through the doors of the debating chamber over the years is wide and varied – from public figures like Winston Churchill, Ronald Reagan, Muammar Gaddafi and the Dalai Lama to scientists like Stephen Hawking and entertainers, including Steven Sondheim, Rupert Everett, Jerry Springer and Pamela Anderson. Until recently, membership was only open to members of the University or Anglia Ruskin, who could attend debates. Now anyone over 18 can apply for Open Membership and enjoy access to selected debates and social events. Or you could soak up the atmosphere when the Cambridge Literary Festival takes up weekend residence twice a year.

Address 9A Bridge Street, CB1 1UB, +44 (0)1223 566421, cus.org | Getting there
Buses 1, 2, 3, 8 or Citi 5 to Bridge Street; Grand Arcade car park | Hours See website
for details of open events | Tip The Orator bar and restaurant (open to all) is a large,
comfortable space inside the Union building. The lovely courtyard garden offers a welcome
break from the hubbub of Bridge Street. Visit their website www.cus.org/the-orator for
opening hours.

107__The University Library

It's not just about books

'What's that building?' is a frequent question from those approaching Cambridge from the west. The tower of the University Library is not what people visiting the city first expect to see. It dominates the Cambridge skyline and is several feet taller than King's College chapel and just short of that of St John's. The University Library was designed by Giles Gilbert Scott and echoes the industrial architecture for which he is best known. Built between 1931 and 1934, the UL, as it's generally known, occupies an eight-acre site previously used as a military hospital in World War I and then as temporary accommodation during the post-war housing shortage.

In 2016, the University Library celebrated the 600th anniversary of its founding by two scholars who bequeathed books to 'the common library of all scholars of the University'. It took 500 years to accumulate its first million books, then the collection expanded enormously and the UL now holds around eight million items. As a UK legal deposit library, it receives nearly 100,000 titles every year – and then there is the digital library for electronic material. Lack of space has become critical and in 2017 work began on an off-site facility in Ely, which will provide 65 miles of storage space by 2025.

All members of the University can borrow 10–20 books for up to 8 weeks, while the library's online catalogue can be accessed by scholars around the world. Readers wanting to consult or borrow a book look up its reference number, fill out a request form and leave it for a book fetcher, who will find it within 20 minutes.

Throughout the year the library puts on exhibitions in a space that is open to the public. However, if you do not manage to visit in person, the UL's website hosts excellent virtual versions that can be accessed long after the physical exhibitions are over. You can navigate the show, zoom into close-ups of the exhibits and expand captions at will.

Address West Road, CB3 9DR, +44 (0)1223 333000, www.lib.cam.ac.uk | Getting there
Bus U to Grange Road, opposite Robinson College | Hours Exhibition Centre (open
to the public) Mon–Fri 9am–6.30pm, Sat 9am–4.30pm; check website for details of
exhibition tours and occasional tower tours | Tip In front of the University Library stand
14 bollards that are also bronze sculptures. Created by Cambridge sculptor Harry Gray, the
bollards are actually columns of books, where the middle four swivel round and together
spell the words *Ex Libris*.

108_ Varsity Hotel Rooftop Bar

360-degree boutique chic

Why was it that the French writer Guy de Maupassant lunched at the Eiffel Tower every day? It was, he told his friends, the only place from where he could not see it – charming and romantic to some, useless and monstrous to others. While the Varsity Hotel might not arouse quite such passions, its construction did provoke strong views about its domination of the Cambridge skyline. Opinions are still divided, but what cannot be denied is that the Varsity is a delightfully appointed hotel, with a roof terrace bar that offers unparalleled views across the city.

Until the 18th century, the area around the Varsity was part of a thriving river trade, where boats brought goods upriver for unloading next to Magdalene Bridge. The whole area was rich in inns, pubs and warehouses; the street names give an indication of its history: Ship Lane and Maltings Lane. The arrival of the railway in 1845 put paid to the trade and the area declined.

The Varsity Hotel, which opened in 2010, is tucked away down a narrow residential street close to the river and city centre and is everything a boutique hotel should be: small (just 48 rooms), chic and stylishly decorated. Its spa and steakhouse are housed in the old Anchor Brewery, redesigned by Conran and Partners.

It's worth ignoring the lift and instead climbing the stairs to the top, just to take in the classy décor and attractive, quirky artwork. On the sixth floor is the Six Panorama Bar and Restaurant, which is a good bet for a drink, afternoon tea or dinner when the Cambridge skies are a leaden grey. But if the day or evening is fine it's worth climbing that last floor to the roof terrace, where the view is even more dazzling, and you can watch the sun set from one of the most romantic spots in the city.

Address Thompson's Lane, CB5 8AQ, +44 (0)1223 306030, www.thevarsityhotel.co.uk | Getting there Citi 5 or 6 to Bridge Street, Grand Arcade car park; valet parking facility available for residents | Hours Mon 5–9pm, Sun–Thu noon–9pm, Fri & Sat noon–10pm, weather permitting; closed during the winter | Tip If you walk towards the river you will come across several punting stations – Let's Go Punting and Rutherford's next to the Italian restaurant La Mimosa and the much larger Scudamore's on Quayside. Any of them can take you on a relaxing and informative tour through the Backs and up to Silver Street.

109_ Wandlebury

Providing a great place to wander
for nearly 3,000 years

In Cambridge's very flat landscape, the ridge of hills to the south of the city stands out, even though its summit, Wandlebury Hill, is only a very modest 243 feet high. The hills are named after two mythical local giants, Gog and Magog, whose marriage was characterised by extreme domestic violence. The stuff of legend, of course, but in times past the giants were invoked as bogeymen to keep naughty children in order.

Today, Wandlebury and the Gogs are part of a peaceful country park that incorporates the remains of an Iron Age hill fort and links with the nearby Roman road that runs towards Suffolk. The site is a mix of unobtrusively managed woodland, ideal for exploring and building dens, and open meadows, full of wildflowers and perfect for picnicking and lazing. You can walk round the Wandlebury Ring, which traces the defences of the ancient hill fort and contains a stable block, all that remains of a stately home that was built in the 18th century and stood until the 1950s, when its poor condition led to demolition. This grand house was the home of the Earl of Godolphin, the owner of the Godolphin Arabian, a famous stallion that is acknowledged to be the ultimate sire of most of the greatest racehorses of the last 275 years. When the horse died, it was given a ceremonial burial. You can visit its grave by the stable block.

The last private owners of Wandlebury, the Gray family, gifted half of the estate to the charity Cambridge Past, Present and Future, which bought the remaining half with funds raised through a public appeal. Over a period of three years, the formal gardens were restyled as open grassland and the site was made safe for visitors, opening to the public in August 1959. The charity now runs a wide variety of nature-based activities and events for all ages throughout the year, and during school holidays. Dogs (on leads) are welcome.

Address Off the A1307, CB22 3AE | **Getting there** Stagecoach bus 13 or 13A; bicycle. Entry is free but there is a charge for the visitors' car park at the site. Alternatively, there is free parking at the Babraham Road Park & Ride 0.5 miles away. | **Tip** The award-winning Gog Magog Farm Shop on the Babraham Road has a butcher, a fresh produce shop and a delicatessen selling delicious cheeses and artisan bread, among other things. The café is open for coffee, cake and lunch.

110_Whipple Museum of the History of Science

Whipping up enthusiasm for science

A museum that describes its own collection as 'eccentric' is irresistible – which is just as well, because when you arrive at the Whipple Museum's entrance it is not immediately inviting. But perhaps this is all part of its eccentricity, because once inside it has more than its fair share of the amazing, absorbing and amusing.

Cambridge's reputation as an entrepreneurial, high-technology centre dates back to the late 19th century when Horace Darwin, Charles Darwin's youngest son, co-founded the Cambridge Scientific Instrument Company. His assistant was Robert Stewart Whipple, who later headed up the company and in due course donated his personal collection of antique scientific instruments to the museum that was named after him.

From the start, the museum was intended to be interactive. The founding committee stipulated, '[I]t is important that the museum should be … designed and maintained as a valuable teaching instrument and a cultural accessory to modern research.' It continues to fulfil this role today. The eclectic range of exhibits includes everything imaginable about the history of science, including papier mâché anatomical models, astronomical apparatus and telescopes that are as much works of art as scientific instruments. Children as well as adults will be delighted to see the large sign encouraging visitors to open the drawers in the Discover section – and anyone old enough to have been offered one as a present or a perk at work will enjoy the calculator display.

The Whipple Museum saves the best till last with a room full of globes on the second floor. Here you will learn the difference between orreries, astrolabes and armillary spheres, and you'll be hard-pressed to choose which you would love to be able to take home.

Address Free School Lane, CB2 3RH, +44 (0)1223 330906, www.sites.hps.cam.ac.uk/whipple | Getting there Any Citi bus (1–8) to town centre; Grand Arcade car park | Hours Mon–Fri 12.30–4.30pm | Tip On the wall of the Engineering Laboratory a little further on in Free School Lane is a memorial plaque to the electrical engineer John Hopkinson, and his son John Gustave, who died on 27 August 1898. What the plaque does not record is that they died in a climbing accident in Switzerland, and that two of Hopkinson's daughters died with them, one of whom, Alice, had just graduated from Newnham College.

111 Xu Zhimo Memorial

The magnetic power of a willow and a white stone

It's not the majesty of King's College Chapel that they come to see, or its sweeping lawns or even the river. The thousands of Chinese visitors who come to Cambridge each year head straight for a large stone close to the bridge that joins Scholar's Piece to the rest of the college. Inscribed on the stone are two verses of a poem by Xu Zhimo, China's most admired modernist poet, taught to all Chinese schoolchildren.

Xu Zhimo wrote *A Second Farewell to Cambridge* in 1928 after a return visit to the city. He first arrived in 1921 to study politics and economics but was captivated by the Romantic poets – Keats, Shelley, Wordsworth and Coleridge – and changed direction, becoming a writer and a poet. He returned to China, inspired to use these western influences and combine them with traditional Chinese verse.

Although famous in China, Xu Zhimo has remained largely unknown outside his own country. His poem refers to 'the golden willows', and when plans were laid to cut one of them down, a member of the college knew enough about him to alert them to its importance and get the scheme stopped. In 2008 a Hong Kong businessman who had been at Cambridge proposed that King's should put up a memorial to China's famous son. The plan was steered through, not without controversy, by the renowned historian Professor Alan Macfarlane, and two years later the stone was ready. Made of white Beijing marble and with calligraphy executed in Xu Zhimo's home town, the poem talks of love and loss, memories and dreams. Like an iceberg, half the stone (which weighs just over two tons) is buried beneath the ground. Ten years later a Chinese garden (the first to be built inside any Cambridge college) was installed just behind the stone, and opened by Xu Zhimo's grandson. It features the traditional yin and yang pattern, and blends together many English and native Chinese plants.

Address King's College, King's Parade, CB2 1ST, +44 (0)1223 331100, www.kings.cam.ac.uk | **Getting there** Bus 119 to Bene't Street; Grand Arcade car park | **Hours** Variable; check at Porters' Lodge | **Tip** Right outside the gates of King's is an original hexagonal Penfold pillar box, first introduced in 1866, with a decorated leaf cap and an acanthus bud on the top.

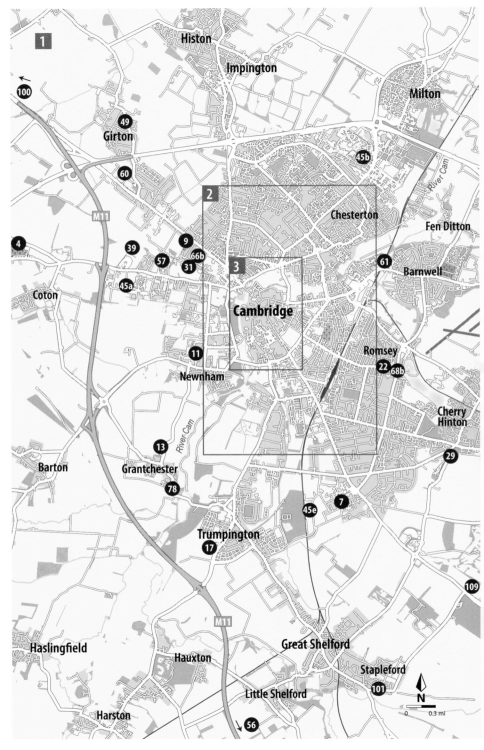

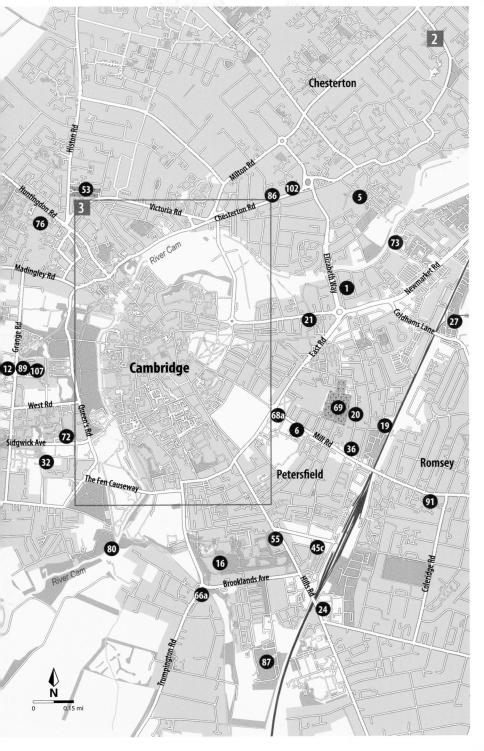

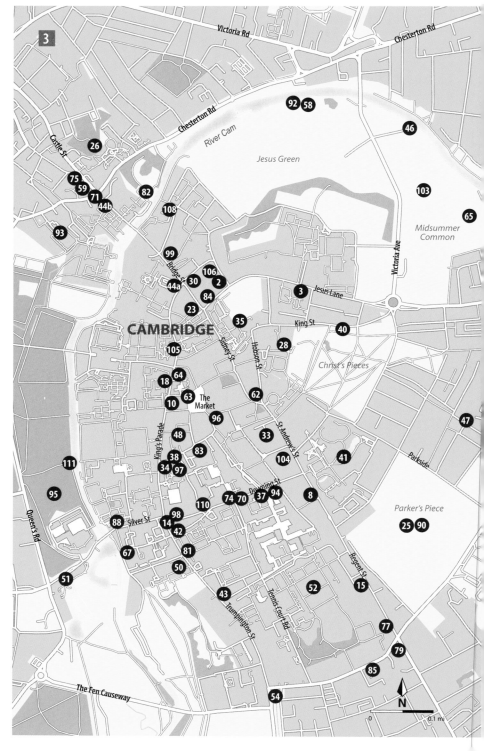

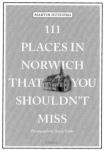

Martin Dunford, Karin Tearle
111 Places in Norwich
That You Shouldn't Miss
ISBN 978-3-7408-1733-6

Ben Waddington, Janet Hart
111 Places in Birmingham
That You Shouldn't Miss
ISBN 978-3-7408-2268-2

Rob Ganley, Ian Williams
111 Places in Coventry
That You Shouldn't Miss
ISBN 978-3-7408-1044-3

Phil Lee, Rachel Ghent
111 Places in Nottingham
That You Shouldn't Miss
ISBN 978-3-7408-2261-3

Ed Glinert, David Taylor
111 Places in Oxford
That You Shouldn't Miss
ISBN 978-3-7408-1990-3

John Sykes, Birgit Weber
111 Places in London
That You Shouldn't Miss
ISBN 978-3-7408-2379-5

Alicia Edwards
111 Places for Kids in London
That You Shouldn't Miss
ISBN 978-3-7408-2196-8

Terry Philpot, Karin Tearle
111 Literary Places in London
That You Shouldn't Miss
ISBN 978-3-7408-1954-5

Michael Glover, Benedict Flett
111 Hidden Art Treasures
in London That You Shouldn't
Miss
ISBN 978-3-7408-1576-9

Jonjo Maudsley, James Riley
111 Places in Windsor
That You Shouldn't Miss
ISBN 978-3-7408-2009-1

Solange Berchemin
111 Places in the Lake District
That You Shouldn't Miss
ISBN 978-3-7408-2404-4

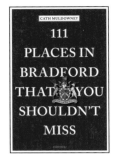

Cath Muldowney
111 Places in Bradford
That You Shouldn't Miss
ISBN 978-3-7408-1427-4

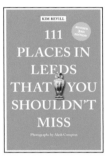

Kim Revill, Alesh Compton
111 Places in Leeds
That You Shouldn't Miss
ISBN 978-3-7408-2059-6

Michael Glover,
Richard Anderson
111 Places in Sheffield
That You Shouldn't Miss
ISBN 978-3-7408-2348-1

Julian Treuherz,
Peter de Figueiredo
111 Places in Manchester
That You Shouldn't Miss
ISBN 978-3-7408-2246-0

Julian Treuherz,
Peter de Figueiredo
111 Places in Liverpool
That You Shouldn't Miss
ISBN 978-3-7408-1607-0

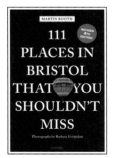

Martin Booth, Barbara Evripidou
111 Places in Bristol
That You Shouldn't Miss
ISBN 978-3-7408-2001-5

Martin Booth, Barbara Evripidou
111 Places for Kids in Bristol
That You Shouldn't Miss
ISBN 978-3-7408-1665-0

Justin Postlethwaite
**111 Places in Bath
That You Shouldn't Miss**
ISBN 978-3-7408-0146-5

Alexandra Loske
**111 Places in Brighton and
Lewes That You Shouldn't Miss**
ISBN 978-3-7408-1727-5

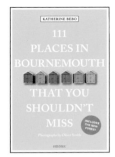

Katherine Bebo, Oliver Smith
**111 Places in Bournemouth
That You Shouldn't Miss**
ISBN 978-3-7408-1166-2

Katherine Bebo, Oliver Smith
**111 Places in Poole
That You Shouldn't Miss**
ISBN 978-3-7408-0598-2

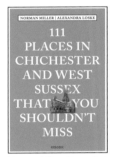

Norman Miller, Alexandra Loske
**111 Places in Chichester
and West Sussex That You
Shouldn't Miss**
ISBN 978-3-7408-1784-8

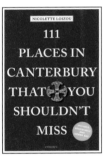

Nicolette Loizou
**111 Places in Canterbury
That You Shouldn't Miss**
ISBN 978-3-7408-0899-0

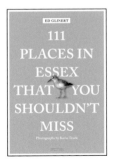

Ed Glinert, Karin Tearle
**111 Places in Essex
That You Shouldn't Miss**
ISBN 978-3-7408-1593-6

Catriona Neil, Adrian Spalding
**111 Places in Cornwall
That You Shouldn't Miss**
ISBN 978-3-7408-1901-9

Ed Glinert, David Taylor
**111 Places in Yorkshire
That You Shouldn't Miss**
ISBN 978-3-7408-1167-9

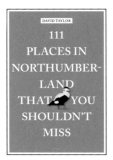

David Taylor
**111 Places in Northumberland
That You Shouldn't Miss**
ISBN 978-3-7408-1792-3

David Taylor
**111 Places in Newcastle
That You Shouldn't Miss**
ISBN 978-3-7408-1043-6

David Taylor
**111 Places along Hadrian's Wall
That You Shouldn't Miss**
ISBN 978-3-7408-1425-0

Gillian Tait
**111 Places in Edinburgh
That You Shouldn't Miss**
ISBN 978-3-7408-1476-2

Tom Shields, Gillian Tait
**111 Places in Glasgow
That You Shouldn't Miss**
ISBN 978-3-7408-2237-8

David Taylor
**111 Places in the Scottish
Highlands That You Shouldn't
Miss**
ISBN 978-3-7408-2064-0

Gillian Tait
**111 Places in Fife
That You Shouldn't Miss**
ISBN 978-3-7408-1740-4

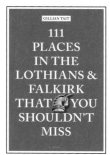

Gillian Tait
**111 Places in the Lothians and
Falkirk That You Shouldn't Miss**
ISBN 978-3-7408-1569-1

Julia Goodfellow-Smith
**111 Places in Swansea
That You Shouldn't Miss**
ISBN 978-3-7408-2065-7

Acknowledgements

We are grateful to the many friends who entered enthusiastically into this project, sharing with us their favourite places and making many helpful suggestions. Their invaluable knowledge and input greatly enriched the contents of this book.

We would like to acknowledge the debt we owe to Allan Brigham (1951–2020), who probably knew more about the city than anyone. His Town Not Gown walking tours of Cambridge were an inspiration and brought the city to life.

We would also like to express our gratitude to those who gave us access and allowed us to photograph. In particular, we thank: The Master and Fellows of Christ's College, Churchill College, Emmanuel College, Gonville and Caius College, Magdalene College, Pembroke College, Sidney Sussex College; The President and Fellows of Queens' College and Wolfson College; The Provost and Scholars of King's College; The Warden and Fellows of Robinson College; Neil Adams, All Saints' Church/Westcott House, Sam Baxter, Lesley Bermingham, Hannah Bicknell, Matt Boucher, Wendy Brown, Charlotte Connelly, Carolin Crawford, David Crilly, Louise Gamon, Greene King, Pam Halls, Nicola Hamilton, Sarah Hammond, Kate Hannah, Canon Harkness, Judith Harrison, Ed Hine, Lauren Hodges, Richard Holmes, Katie Hook, Katharine Horbury, Anthony Hyde, Sylwester Iwaniec, David Jarvis, Angela and Toby Joseph, Kees Ludekens, Eric Marland, Canon Nick Moir, Heidi Mulvey, Helen Needham, George Pearson, Sally Petitt, Roberto Pintus, Patrice Pollet, Andy Powell, Isaac Reed, Emin Refioglu, David Richards, Kate Romano, Jethro Scotcher-Littlechild, James Smith, Rachel Rose Smith, Jeremy Thackray, Jack Toye, Susanne Turner, Tarquin Ukarnis, Claire Wallace, Heidi White, Tamsin Wimhurst and Charlotte Woodley.

Ros Horton was brought up and studied in London but moved to Cambridge to pursue a career in publishing. After many years in educational marketing at Cambridge University Press she left to work freelance, and reinvented herself as an editor. Getting together with her former colleague and friend of over 30 years, Sally Simmons, they formed Cambridge Editorial and worked together for many years. She enjoys singing, and has recently started organising singing workshops. She has played the ukulele for a number of years, including with *The Misspent Ukes* and *Major Swing*, a hot-club style jazz band.

Sally Simmons was one of only 25 female undergraduates to go up to Sidney Sussex College when it first admitted women in 1976. She began her career in publishing at Cambridge University Press, where Ros Horton was her first boss. Marriage took her to France for several years, where she started her family and became a committed Francophile. She now divides her time between Cambridge and Fontainebleau and continues to write and edit on the move.

Guy Snape was born in North Staffordshire and studied at Birmingham, Kingston and Cambridge universities. In a varied career, he has been a schoolteacher in the UK and Greece, a software consultant, and a music teacher, following which he retrained as a counsellor and hypnotherapist and now runs a successful private practice. He lives in Cambridge with his wife and their two children, plus cat and dog.

The information in this book was accurate at the time of publication, but it can change at any time. Please confirm the details for the places you're planning to visit before you head out on your adventures.